A to Z Missouri:

The dictionary of Missouri Place Names

"How interesting! Reading about the pioneer days in Missouri, I'm seeing our towns and cities in a whole new light. . . ."

Phillip Ratterman
Modern day explorer
Kansas City, Mo

A to Z Missouri:

The dictionary of Missouri Place Names

Compiled by
Margot Ford McMillen

With a foreword by Kenneth Winn,
Director of Missouri State Archives

Illustrations by Dennis Murphy

Pebble Publishing
Columbia, Missouri

7

JUNE 27, 2008

Project support by Pebble Publishing staff:
Brett Dufur, Daisy Dufur, Pippa Letsky and Heather Starek

ISBN 0-9646625-4-X 14.95
Copyright © 1996 by Margot Ford McMillen
All other rights © 1996 by Pebble Publishing

Pebble Publishing, P.O. Box 431, Columbia, MO 65205-0431
Phone: (573) 698-3903 Fax: (573) 698-3108
E-Mail: pebble@global-image.com

Printed by Ovid Bell Press, Fulton, Missouri, USA

Dedicated to

Everyone who has
ever been delighted by
the story behind a place name.

Other Books in the Show Me Missouri Series:

99 Fun Things To Do In Columbia and Boone County

Best of Missouri Hands

Exploring Missouri Wine Country

Famous Missourians Who Made History

Forgotten Missourians Who Made History

The Complete Katy Trail Guidebook

What's That? A Nature Guide to the Missouri River Valley

Wit and Wisdom of Missouri's Country Editors

Contents

Foreword

The force of local tradition will prevail . . .

A few years ago, my friend Rebecca Schroeder suggested that I put together a dictionary-style listing of Missouri place names. She told me that a Kansas publisher had produced such manuals for several states. My husband, Howard Marshall, and I were looking for a project to do together and we soon had a start on it, but when we sent our list to the Kansan he wanted to cut some of our best stuff. He said, for example, that Ella Ewing Lake couldn't be named for an 8'4" tall woman. He said she must have been shorter because she wasn't in the Guinness Book of World Records. He wanted facts.

The Kansan wanted to know the geology of the mud in the Mississippi River at Cape Girardeau. What made it greasy enough to earn the nickname "Greasy Cove"? And how about Missouri's six Greasy Creeks? What made them so slippery? He asked where the young braves at Arrow Rock stood to shoot their arrows across the river. On the bluff? In the water? He even doubted some place name stories collected by students of Robert Ramsay, professor of English at the University of Missouri-Columbia from 1907-1951. We don't know if the tales in the Ramsay file tell the truth about place names, but we know they are stories that Missourians love.

It was enough to make weaker folks give up, move to a farm and raise emus for a living. Because the truth about place names is carried by what the people think, and not necessarily by the facts. Everyone in Scotland County, for example, knows how tall Ella Ewing was. They've heard from aunts and uncles that the doors of Miss Ella's house were nine feet tall, and how her hair brushed the lintels. People remember her funeral, the enormous casket, and the turnout of friends and curiosity seekers. A souvenir plate documents the event in black and white porcelain—what more proof do you want?

And everyone on the Mississippi River knows the mud's greasy. In the 1920s and 1930s, Americans danced to, whistled and belted out "It's a treat to beat your feet in the Mississippi Mud" from the Barris Cavanaugh classic "Mississippi Mud." The tune was recorded by Bix Beiderbecke, Paul Whiteman, Bob Crosby, Bobby Darin and, most recently, the Muppets, but geology is not the point. Collective memory and generations of tradition—that's the point.

The advice from the Kansan was well-meaning. He wanted to publish a truthful volume about Missouri place names. So we spent long days and sleepless nights worrying over how to make this book accurate. Howard gave up in frustration and used his time more wisely, finishing his book on Nevada architecture and producing new works on Missouri and Scotland.

Joined by researchers Tina Hubbs and Holly and Heather Roberson, I set out to read as many sources as possible. We used the files and collections at the State Historical Society of Missouri, the Western Historical Manuscript Collection and the private collections of friends. When we found two stories, we wrote them both down. We thought we would find a way to separate the true from the false, and then we could toss out the inaccuracies. There were a few times when we thought we had the complete answer on a name, then we'd read another source and there'd be another, entirely new explanation.

I reviewed my oral history files. Looking at my past research, I looked for patterns of truthful versus untruthful place name stories, to use like a pattern to separate stories. I had done research on place names for the Missouri Department of Conservation. I had spoken to many of the men on the naming committee. But even just a few years after voting, they couldn't remember exactly why all the names had been given.

A few clear images stuck with them, like the gay feather flowers blooming on Gay Feather Prairie, but other images had faded. One namer told me that Birdsong Prairie was named for a family, another told me it was named for the birds singing the morning they went to visit, another told me it was the name of a branch of the Osage tribe. The naming committee kept no written records, so where was the truth?

Finally, we saw the light.

Nobody can produce a book that tells only the accurate stories about place names exactly as they happened. Some names are given thoughtfully, by people who record the process. Others simply evolve, accumulating stories after the fact. Our motto became: "The force of local tradition will prevail."

Place name stories bind a community together. Like other family stories, the place name story says, "We're special. Our place is unique." The story may prove that we're brave or historic or have a sense of humor but, like other family history, it doesn't particularly matter whether others think it is true.

Indeed, the stories tell more about the teller than they do about the place. Maries River is a good example. This name, which I believe is a corrupted form of, *marais*, French for "swamp," has produced other stories. Some people think the name honors two little girls, both named Mary, who drowned in the river. After my book <u>Paris, Tightwad and Peculiar</u> (University of Missouri Press, 1994) came out, I received a letter from a priest who wrote I had "touched some raw nerves." He was sure the name was given by early French explorers for the Virgin Mary.

As a student of the subject, I stuck with the "marais" explanation. If you live in the area, you may want to stick with the two little girls. As a priest, this gentleman was convinced his explanation was right.

So, this guide presents truths and traditions about place names and place name history. I present it as a book of entertainment rather than scholarship, and I am grateful to Brett Dufur and Pebble Publishing for understanding. If there are mistakes here, blame me or blame local tradition— that wondrous glue that holds together everyday life.

The sources and references used in compiling this book are listed on the back inside cover. Sources, such as (VR), appear after an entry, meaning that the story came from Charles Van Ravenswaay's <u>WPA Guide to Missouri</u>. There are many sources designated as (LI), or local informant. Usually, these contributions have come from local history publications, conversations or articles.

Much of the information marked (LI) has come from friends who explore the subject. Rebecca and Adolf Schroeder and Don Lance have been especially generous with their information and deserve special mention. Conversations with them have refreshed and renewed me countless times.

Finally, let's say you're looking for the origin of your favorite place name and it's not here, or there's something different than what you've always heard. Rise up, dear friend. Write down your story and send it to me at P.O. Box 1762, Columbia, MO 65205. This work will never be done. We'll add new entries to the collection for a future edition.

Margot Ford McMillen

Introduction

Given the polyglot that is New York and the ideological extravaganza that is California, Missouri is probably not the first state that comes to mind when the fashionable concept of "diversity" is mentioned. Still, from the time of its first European settlement through to the first century of its statehood, Missouri served as a cultural crossroads of the nation. The word "Missouri" is derived from the name given the Native Americans who inhabited the region by their Illinois Indian rivals. The French, coming in the seventeenth and eighteenth centuries, adopted the name, simplified it, and gave it to the large river flowing through the area. Westering Americans coming in the nineteenth century gave it to the state they created in 1820. The French added other names of their own, bestowing on us St. Louis, Ste. Genevieve, and St. Joseph, followed by Spanish rulers, who were flattered by ambitious Americans (New Madrid) and whose San Carlos and El Camino Real (St. Charles and Kingshighway) were later anglicized.

Following the Louisiana Purchase in 1803, immigrants from the older regions of the United States began naming Missouri counties after the nation's first heroes–Washington, Jefferson, Madison—in the eastern part of the state, followed by the popular politicians of a later date–Jackson, Clay, Webster, in western Missouri. They brought a fondness for the homes they left behind–Lexington, Richmond, Bowling Green—and the things they valued–Independence, Liberty, Union. By the 1830s some of those heroes were German (Hermann), and later, the counties and cities left behind were Irish (Kerry Patch), Serbian (Belgrade) and Scottish (Edinburg).

These immigrants found rivers that were White, Black, Blue, and Salt; they named the land for the animals they had seen–Elk, Wolf, Buffalo, Fox, Possum, Gopher, and Snake; and their towns for their wives, daughters, and sweethearts–Alice, Emma, Lula, Sedalia, and Vera.

Missouri's imperial enthusiasms are evident in its counties and towns named Texas, Oregon, Taos, Mexico, California, and later the place names of Cuba and Pershing. The state's tragic involvement with slavery and the hope of the new freemen was found in Saline County's Pennytown and Pike's Little Africa.

Though the need for new place names slowed as Missouri matured, our need to identify our state with things important to us continues on today—as exemplified by the recent renaming of Northeast Missouri State University as Truman State—and so it shall forever.

While some of Missouri's creeks are Loose, its Dixie Little, and its towns Peculiar, discovery of the state's varied names is not only occasionally Useful, but quite often Pleasant.

We are, accordingly, in Margot McMillen's debt for offering us hours of diversion in the listing of the thirteen hundred or so place names that follow below and, far more importantly, for her insight and cleverness in showing us how we came to be.

Kenneth H. Winn
Director of Missouri State Archives

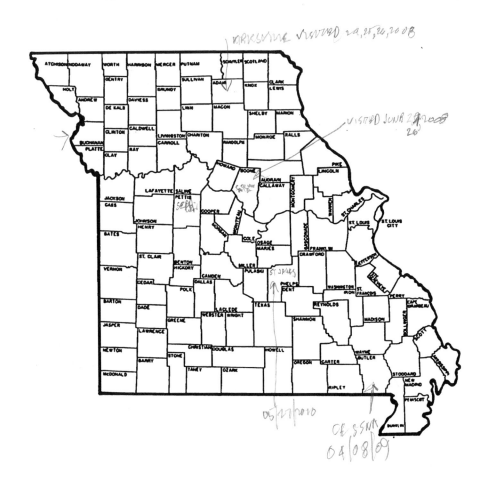

KIRKSVILLE VISITED 24, 25, 26, 2008

VISITED JUNE 29, 2008
26

05/27/2010

CE SSM
04/08/09

Aberdeen [ab uhr DEEN] (Pike). A Virginian of Scottish descent settled here and accumulated 13,000 acres. With that much land, he could name it whatever he wanted, and he chose the name of the Scottish city. The property could only be entered by passing through a tollgate, around which grew a village. When the village applied for a post office, the name was adopted (RF). P.O. 1871-1879, 1890-1907.

Abo [AY boh] (Laclede). This fishing resort was named by a mill owner, who thought he was giving it an Indian name for house or home (RF). There was another Abo in McDonald County (RF). P.O. (McDonald) 1882-1886, (Laclede) 1893-1940.

Acme Heights (St. Louis). This part of St. Louis is named for the Greek word meaning a point, height, summit (RF).

Adair County [uh DAIR]. Named for John Adair, a governor of Kentucky. This name is a reminder of the southern roots of many Missourians. See Little Dixie. When the cornerstone for the new courthouse was laid in 1898, it was reported that 15,000 people attended. This was during the Spanish-American War, and Cuban flags were displayed side by side with Old Glory (MO). Organized 1841. Pop. 24,577.

Adam-ondi-Ahman (Daviess). A shrine marks the sacred ground where this Mormon town was thriving in the 1830s when Gallatin, now county seat, was a scraggly row of three saloons and seven houses. Built by hundreds of Joseph Smith's followers after they were chased from the Independence area, the name was revealed to Smith as meaning "Adam's Consecrated Land" in "the Reformed Egyptian language" (VR) because, Smith said, Adam had lived there after his exile from Paradise (GS). The name was shortened to Di-amon, Diamong or Diamond (RF).

Adrian [AY dree uhn] (Bates). This name may have been given by persons who came from Adrian, Michigan (VR), but a more likely story is that it was named for one of the four sons of the general passenger agent of the Missouri Pacific Railroad. He is responsible also for Archie (Cass), Arthur (Vernon) and Sheldon (Vernon) (RF). P.O. 1880-now. Pop. 1,582.

Advance City [AD vans] (Stoddard). According to the Dexter Statesman (1928), this name was given in 1910 when the Houck Railroad advanced the road one mile past its existing terminus. If the post office date is correct, this story is in error. P.O. 1882-now. Pop. 1,139.

Agency (Buchanan). The U.S. Government Agency for the Sac and Fox Indians was located here, long before the town was founded (Enc). P.O. 1872-now. Pop. 642.

Airline Junction (Jackson). This railroad station derived its name from the fact that the branch line of the railroad is very straight here—as straight as an air line (RF).

Albany [AWL buh nee] (Gentry) county seat. Laid off in 1845 and named Athens, the town was renamed because there was another town in the state named Athens. The new name was suggested by a settler for the capital of his native state, New York (RF). P.O. 1857-now. Pop. 1,958.

Alexandria (Clark). (1) When the first ferryman, John Alexander, built his cabin here, there was no settlement. Later, his name was given to the village that grew up at this natural boat landing (RF). (2) This is a "classical name" from the "empire-building" era (VR). See Antioch. From 1847 to 1854, this was the county seat, but repeated flooding forced removal to the inland site of Kahoka. P.O. 1841-now. Pop. 341.

Altamont [AL thu mahnt] (Daviess). From the Latin-derived *alta* (high) and *mont* (mountain), this town has an elevation of 1,002 feet at the railroad depot (Enc). P.O. 1890-now. Pop. 188.

Altenburg [AL tuhn buhrg] (Perry). Of five Perry county towns established by some of Missouri's first German Lutheran immigrants in 1839, three survive. The story of the immigration is dramatic: 700 settlers left on five ships, fleeing religious and economic persecution. One ship was lost at sea, the others landed in New Orleans and the survivors progressed to Missouri, partly inspired by Duden's book (see Duden's Hill). Altenburg, named for the Duchy of Saxe-Altenburg, home of most of the settlers, had an academy for men and women. (See Dresden, Frohna, Seelitz, Wittenberg.) P.O. 1854-now. Pop. 256.

Alton (Oregon) county seat. The first postmaster in this town came from Alton, Illinois, hence the name. People have found other explanations, however. One story goes that the name All Town was chosen because the three citizens appointed to select the name decided to name it for all of themselves. Another explanation is that the original name was "Awl Town," associated with the craft of shoemaking (RF). P.O. 1860-now. Pop. 692.

Amarugia (Cass). This region, which stretches between the Bates County border, Archie, Everett and Main City, is rich with local lore. Natives say it once proclaimed itself a kingdom, complete with king, buried treasure and angry, long-lived feuds among the citizens. Origins for the name are obscure: It may have been an adaptation of *ambrosia*, Greek for "Food of the Gods." Another theory: The word is supposed to mean "distasteful," or "bitter," in a Native American dialect (LI).

Amazonia [am uh ZOHN yuh] or [am uh ZOH nee uh] (Andrew). First named Nodaway City, the name was changed to Boston, and then to Amazonia (CG). No explanation could be found for the name. Maybe the founders were reading about the Amazon River, comparing it to the Mississippi. Maybe they just liked the way "Amazonia" sounds. P.O. 1859-1865, 1867-now. Pop. 257.

"America's Main Street." This is a nickname for Highway 66, which passed through St. Louis, Rolla, Joplin and Springfield on its way from Chicago to the Santa Monica pier (LI).

Americus
Arbela

Americus [uh MER i kuhs] (Montgomery). Named for a town in Georgia, this town was surveyed just as the county was recovering from the Civil War. P.O. 1867-1959.

Andrew County [AN droo]. This county was a part of the Platte Purchase and was named in honor of Andrew Jackson Davis, a prominent lawyer of St. Louis and formerly of Savannah, the county seat (RF). Another story theorizes the county was named after popular Andrew Jackson, whose last name and nickname had already been used in Jackson and Hickory Counties (LI). See Jackson County. Organized 1841. Pop. 14,632.

Antioch (Taney, Clark). Roman history was taught in American elementary schools until quite recently and allusions to the classics were part of our culture. So, Missouri has a number of towns named by postmasters and citizens remembering their education. Scholars have remarked on this phenomenon: Van Ravenswaay calls it a "classical name popular in the empire-building era" (VR). The daughter of James Fennimore Cooper put it this way: "After the Revolution came the direful invasion of the ghosts of old Greeks and Romans headed by the Yankee Schoolmaster with an Abridgement of Ancient History in his pocket. It was then your Troys and Uticas, your Tullys and Scipios, your Romes and Palmyras, your Homers and Virgils, were dropped about the country in scores" (RF). P.O. 1879, 1883-1907.

Antonia (Jefferson). First named Bulltown because cattle here clogged the road to St. Louis, the name was changed to honor a local merchant, Antoine Yeager (LI). Around the turn of the century, a bloody family feud here made the neighborhood dance halls and honky tonks notorious.

Anutt [AN uht] (Dent). This name was suggested by the pupil of a schoolteacher named Miss Annet Lenox (RF). Spelling was not his best subject. P.O. 1890-1963. Pop. 60.

Arbela [ahr BEE luh] (Scotland). Two choices: (1) Perhaps the only town in the United States by this name, Arbela's namesake is Arbil in Asia, the site of a famous battle in 381 B.C. (RF). (2) This was named for a town in Scotland (Enc). It was first known as Perryville, Burnt Church or Burnt Shirt, and there are two stories attached to the name Burnt Shirt. (1) A railroad construction man lost his shirt to a brush fire. (2) A card player set his shirt on fire to make a torch so the game could be finished after dark (RF). P.O. 1852-now. Pop. 40.

Arbyrd [AER buhrd] (Dunklin). This name is the combination of A.R. Byrd, a prominent citizen (RF). P.O. 1911-now. Pop. 597.

Archangel Access (Schuyler). This Department of Conservation property is part of the old home place of Henry Clay Dean, a famous pro-southern orator during the Civil War (LI). Dean was "An Archangel," according to Mark Twain's Life on the Mississippi. "When Dean came," Twain quoted an informant, "the people thought he was an escaped lunatic; but when he left they thought he was an escaped archangel."

Archie [AHR chee] (Cass). See Adrian. P.O. 1880-now. Pop. 799.

Argonne [AHR gawn] (Lafayette). This train stop was known as Hall's Station, but was renamed after the Americans won a battle at the forest of Argonne (RF).

Argyle [AHR geyel] (Maries-Osage). According to a local story, this town was named by a conductor who got tired of calling out "St. Boniface," the official town name. He just blurted out "Argyle" one day and it stuck (LI). Unfortunately, this great story probably isn't true. The town was named by John Connor, a farmer in the neighborhood, for Argyllshire or Argyll in Scotland (RF). P.O. 1904-now. Pop. 178.

Arkoe [AHR koh] (Nodaway). Although the town's founder claimed this name comes from Jules Verne's Twenty Thousand Leagues Under the Sea, the name does not appear there (RF). It comes from Robert Paltock's Peter Wilkins (GS). P.O. 1877-1953.

Arrow Rock (Saline). Founded as a trading post in 1808, almost everyone heading west passed through this area. A natural river crossing, it was used in early times by Native Americans as a meeting place. According to one story, the name marks an event when a group of young men were competing to win the chief's daughter. The contest involved shooting arrows to see which brave was strongest. The winning archer shot his arrow all the way across the Missouri River into a rock on the other side (LI). The French called the place Pierre a Fleche, French for "Arrow Rock." In 1829, when Americans decided to build here, they chose the name New Philadelphia. This name never caught on, and Arrow Rock got its old name back (RF). P.O. 1821-now. Pop. 70.

Native American Place Names

I t would seem that the Missouri landscape should sport hundreds of place names given by the Osage and Missouri Indians, the two nations living here when Europeans first came. Of those Osage and Missouri names, we should expect dozens more that hark back to earlier populations. Alas, there are not. Only a small number of natives lived here when the Europeans came, and there was little interaction between the groups. No prehistoric names pepper our maps.

While seven Missouri counties bear "Indian names," none were used as place names by tribes who lived here. The old waterway names Wakenda and Niangua were proposed as county names, but were changed to Carroll and Dallas. Wakenda, a name for the Deity, appears in many spellings including Wyaconda. Niangua seems a combination of *ni*, meaning "river," with a modifier *angua*, but we are not sure of the exact meaning.

Some of the Native American names that we use—like Hoozaw, Huzzah, Whosau and Osage—are American and French attempts to spell a Native American word. Others—like Bon Homme, Bonne Femme and Femme Osage—are French names given for Native American people. Still others—like Black Hawk, Pocahontas and Tecumseh—are American names of people much romanticized and admired in the American press and by American writers.

Some place names, like Missouri, were written down by explorers from the language of their guides. These guides may have been Native Americans, but were not usually Osage or Missouri. See Missouri for more information. Some names came much later, with tribes evacuated from the east on the Trail of Tears. Still others came west with American settlers from eastern states.

A double handful of our place names are associated with "Indian legends." Arrow Rock, Marais des Cygnes, Mina Sauk Falls, Creve Coeur Lake and a number of Lovers' Leaps are supposedly the sites of legendary Indian events. While we cannot be sure when

these legends were born, they have European counterparts in ballads
and stories hundreds of years old. Indeed, these "Indian legends"
seem to be universal stories, the embodiment of ageless human romantic yearning put into words.

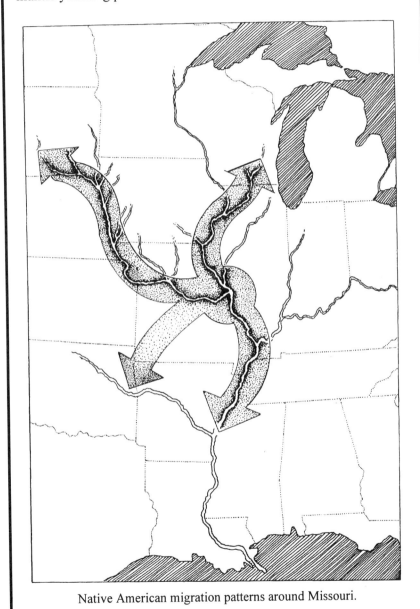

Native American migration patterns around Missouri.

Arthur (Vernon). See Adrian. P.O. 1880-now.

Ashland (Boone). The town of Farmer's Corner adopted this name in 1853, to honor Henry Clay, who died a year earlier (APM). See Clay County. Ashland was the name of Clay's estate in Lexington, Kentucky (RF). A less likely story is that the name may have also been for a grove of ash trees near the town (RF). P.O. 1856-now. Pop. 1,252.

Ashley Cave (Texas). This cave was used by William Henry Ashley, a fur trader and first lieutenant governor of the state. The name was taken by a nearby post office.

Atchison County [ACH uh suhn]. This county was named in honor of David R. Atchison, who was at the time a pro-slavery Democrat and U.S. senator from Missouri (RF). Through a technicality, Atchison became president for one day in March 1849, when there was a delay in inaugurating Zachary Taylor (DM). Organized 1845. Pop. 7,457.

Athens [AY thuhnz] (Clark). See Albany and Antioch. P.O. 1884-1922.

Audrain County [aw DRAYN] or [AW drayn]. Named for James Audrain, pioneer of St. Charles County and member of the state legislature of the Eighth District from 1830 until his death on November 10, 1831 (RF). Organized 1836. Pop. 23,599.

Auglaize Creek [AW glayz] or [OH glayz]. This many-branched stream was named for the quality of its mud, but the exact meaning of the old Mississippi French word is vague. It first meant "clay mud that could be used for pottery," but the word changed slightly to mean "mud with salt in it," such as was used by animals for salt licks (RF). Its variants appear in many places near Lake of the Ozarks, most notably as Grand Glaize or Grand Glaze.

Augusta [uh GUSS tuh] (St. Charles). First named Mount Pleasant, upon applying for a post office the town changed its name to honor the German founder's wife, as the name Mount Pleasant was already in use (RF). The town was founded in 1836 by Leonard Harold, one of Daniel Boone's followers to St. Charles County, and became settled predominantly by German homesteaders. Until 1872, Augusta was a popular riverboat landing known as Augusta Bend. It was in this year that flooding of the Missouri River caused the river to fill in its main channel, changing its course and cutting Augusta off from the river. Fortunately for the town, the railroad was soon to follow (BD). P.O. 1841-now. Pop. 263.

Aurora [aw ROH ruh] (Lawrence). This name, which reminds the romantic of the Goddess of Dawn, was used by post offices in St. Clair, Platte and Clay Counties before its present site. In 1906, Aurora campaigned to be capital of the United States on the grounds that "there is no fairer spot on the American continent" and that the present capital is too far east (Rayburn's Ozark Guide, 1961). P.O. 1868-now. Pop. 6,459.

Auxvasse [uh VAWZ] or [oh VAWZ] (Callaway). The town is named for the creek, which was named by a party of Frenchmen who traveled with Lilburn Boggs, before he was governor of Missouri. As they tried to cross the creek, they got stuck in mud and named the river *Riviere aux Vases*, which translates to "River of Mud" (DE). The spelling was later corrupted by Americans who did not speak French to Aux Vasse (VR). Locals translate the French to "miry places" (LI). In 1805, a Lewis and Clark map noted "Muddy River," an Americanization of the French name. P.O. 1874-now. Pop. 821.

Ava [AY vuh] (Douglas) county seat. First the site of a Federal Army encampment called Military Springs during the Civil War, Ava was named and laid out in 1871 by James Hailey. He named it Ava from a verse in the Bible (2nd Kings 17:24). Citizens of the Biblical city were moved by the King. The name was also explained thus: *Ava* was said to be Hebrew for "overthrowing," a reference to Ava's "overthrowing" competition for the county seat. To establish the site as county seat, commissioners stole the county records from the old courthouse in Vera Cruz and brought them to Ava (RF). P.O. 1872-now. Pop. 2,938.

Avalon (Livingston). In Celtic mythology, there is an island where the dead go to live eternally in bliss. The hero King Arthur was taken there to die, and would return some day to rescue his people. This is "the blessed isle" where it does not hail, rain or snow (LI). P.O. 1872-now. Pop. 50.

Avenue City (Andrew). In 1877, it was thought that the town of St. Joseph would grow toward Savannah. This town, between the two, was named because it would soon be part of an avenue between (RF). P.O. 1878-1913. Pop. 50.

Avert (Stoddard). This station was named Day, for an early settler, but the name was officially taken by a post office in Taney County. The government gave Avert its name, supposedly to avert confusion (RF). P.O. 1890-1918, 1922-1945.

B

06/27/08

Bado (Texas). This town was established during the Civil War—the bad years (RF).

Bagnell [BAG nel] (Miller). The name of a railroad contractor, this Missouri Pacific Railroad town was also the site of a ferry landing (RF). P.O. 1884-1942. Pop. 89.

Bagnell Dam. See Bagnell. In 1929, Union Electric began building its dam on the Osage River. The dam holds back the Lake of the Ozarks, and provides enough electricity for 225,000 households. Today, the main industry here is tourism (VR).

Bald Joe Mountain (Stone). In 1806, Joe Philibert came down the James River in a canoe with two members of the Delaware tribe and camped at the bottom of this bald knob mountain.

Bald Knob. There are hills known as "Bald Knob" for their bare summits in at least five Missouri counties (RF).

Bald Knobbers' Cave (Christian). This cave, southwest of Chadwick, was a hideout for the vigilante gang, the Baldknobbers, who raged through the Ozarks. Inside, it is spacious, with several rooms and hallways, and a spring of pure water (Hartman and Ingenthron, Baldknobbers).

Barry County [BAIR ee]. This county was named to honor William T. Barry, the first postmaster general of the United States (RF). Barry was a member of President Jackson's cabinet; the county was named when Jackson-naming frenzy was at an all-time high among Missouri Democrats. Organized 1835. Pop. 27,547.

Barton County
Bear Cave

Barton County. This county was named for U.S. Senator David Barton, who was elected as one of Missouri's first two senators on October 2, 1820, in a joint session of the legislature on first ballot. He served until 1830 (RF). Organized 1855. Pop. 11,312.

Bates County [BAYTS]. There is a controversy over the question whether Bates County was named for Frederick Bates, Missouri's second governor, or for his brother Edward Bates, attorney general of the United States under Lincoln (1860-1864). Evidence favors the governor (RF). During the Civil War, this was one of the counties evacuated by Order Number 11, a war act of the Union to rid the countryside of southern sympathizers. When citizens returned, their homes, shop buildings and courthouse had been burned. In a few years, most of the major buildings had been rebuilt (MO). Organized 1841. Pop. 15,025.

Batesville (Bates). Named for the county, the United Foreign Missionary Society of New York established Harmony Mission here in 1821, the year of Missouri statehood, to Christianize the Osage. Osage Chief White Hair and six other Osage chiefs, believing that Osage children needed an education, traveled to Washington, D.C., and asked President Monroe for the mission and donated the land (DM). Forty-one missionary volunteers went to the settlement, including a carpenter, a shoemaker, farmers, a wagon maker and a minister with all their wives and children (VR). When the Osage nation was moved by the government, the missionaries moved with it (LI).

Bear Cave. Even though the black bear is rare (but not extinct) in this state, at least five of our caves are called Bear Cave, because of bears or bear tracks found nearby in the early days of exploration and settlement. These five are located in Camden, Ozark, Gasconade, Franklin and Crawford Counties (RF).

Bear Creek. Further reminders of the black bear in Missouri, there are Bear Creeks in Adair, Boone, Cedar, Clark, Henry, Johnson, Laclede, Lewis, Lincoln, Marion, Miller, Montgomery, Platte, Polk, Ralls, St. Francois, Ste. Genevieve, Scotland, Warren, Wayne and Worth Counties. Lewis County settlers boasted that any day they could go out and kill a "bar" for breakfast (RF).

Beaver Creek. Phelps, Taney and Wayne Counties have Beaver Creeks. Besides being noteworthy for their fauna, these creeks were famous for changing course because of their many dams (RF).

Bee (Cape Girardeau). Unlike most of the "Bee" place names (see Bee Creek), this was probably named for the postmaster—C.B. Davis, who used his middle initial as a nickname (RF).

Bee Creek (Taney). Creeks, ridges and roads in several counties, and this Taney County town, recall days when bees were important to the economy. The honeybee is a European import; Native Americans called them "the white man's fly." Hunting for bees that had escaped their keepers and colonized in the wild was a source of livelihood in pioneer days. Early writers described bee trees that yielded 50 gallons of honey apiece; honey and beeswax were principal exports for some settlements (RF). An Iowa-Missouri border war, The Honey War, was ignited when a Missourian cut down bee trees in the area claimed by both states. P.O. 1871, 1873.

Bee Creek Mills (Platte). See Bee Creek. P.O. 1840-1849.

Belleview (Iron). This was originally named Cross Roads, because it was on the intersection of the Ironton-Caledonia Road and the Iron Mountain-Salem-Springfield Road. When the post office was established in 1876, the name was changed. Belleview is a version of the American restatement of the French regional name—Bellevue Valley (RF). P.O. 1860-now. Pop. 290.

Bellflower (Montgomery). This town was named after a variety of apple (DE). It was named for the small pink flowers that grew there in profusion (RF). It was named for little blue bell-shaped flowers that grew in the prairie grass (LI). P.O. 1887-now. Pop. 413.

Beloit
Bethany

Beloit (Barton). Unlike in most of Missouri, many northerners settled in this spot. They first called this place Carleton Station, then Boston for the city in Massachusetts, then Beloit, probably indicating they came from Wisconsin (LI). P.O. 1881-1891.

Belton (Cass). This name is a combination in the British style—Belt's Town. Mr. Belt, a railway blacksmith had a forge here (RF). P.O. 1872-now. Pop. 18,150.

Bennett Spring State Park (Dallas and Laclede). This state fish hatchery is one of Missouri's most popular trout-fishing areas, famous for elbow-to-elbow opening-day crowds. The spring itself discharges 96 million gallons of cold water every day. The spring and the park are named for W.S. Bennett, who owned the land when the Department of Conservation park was founded in 1923.

Benton [BEN tn] (Scott) county seat. In the early 1850s a developer made this subdivision and named it The Glades, a descriptive name (LI). About 1852 when the Missouri Pacific Railroad was built, the station was named Benton in honor of Thomas Hart Benton (RF). See Benton County. The county seat was first here, then moved to Commerce, then returned to Benton by popular vote (VR). P.O. 1823-1864, 1867-now. Pop. 575.

Benton City (Audrain). Originally known as Jefftown for Jefferson F. Jones, who brought the railroad through, the name was changed in 1881, in honor of Senator Thomas Hart Benton (RF). See Benton County. P.O. 1869-now. Pop. 139.

Benton County. Thomas Hart Benton (1782-1858), one of Missouri's first two senators, served in the 19th century. The colorful and opinionated Benton was elected before there were political parties, but was later a founder of Missouri's Democratic party, an advocate of the western movement and of replacing election by the electoral college with election by popular vote of the citizens. Organized 1835. Pop. 13,859. See also Missouri, The Bullion State.

Bethany (Harrison) county seat. Carthage and Bethany were both proposed as town names. Bethany received the most votes (RF). In the Bible, Bethany was visited frequently by Jesus (LI). Pop. 3,005.

Bethel [BETH l] (Shelby). Founded by a group of 500 German followers of William Keil, Bethel was the name of the first stop on the migration of the Biblical Abraham. The Missouri Germans built a house for each family; single adults lived in a big house, which also served as a hotel. The settlers shared 3,500 acres, which were farmed by the men. The community lasted until 1879, even though Keil left in 1854. P.O. 1848-now. Pop. 117.

Bevier [buh VEER] (Macon). This coal-mining town was named for another coal-mining town in Muhlenberg County, Kentucky. P.O. 1858-1860, 1863-now. Pop. 643.

Big Lake (Holt). Originally called Fish Lake, this lake was named for its size. The lake was once the home of Reazon Bowie, inventor of the famous knife (RF). Pop. 170.

Big Oak Tree State Park (Mississippi). A giant oak tree here, also called Hunter's Oak, was a well-known meeting place for hunters (LI). When the 1904 Louisiana Exposition committee offered a prize for a slice of the biggest tree in Missouri, Big Oak was threatened. As the lumber company began to lay rail for a train to pull Big Oak out of the forest, a group of locals stalled for time, argued and finally raised money to save the giant. The tree survived until the 1950s, when it died a natural death (LI).

Big Piney River (Phelps and Pulaski). Named for the forests that lined its creeks, this river and its Piney tributaries (Piney Creek, Piney Fork, Piney River and Little Piney Creek) have given their names to numerous spots in this area (RF).

Big River (Iron, Jefferson, St. Francois, Washington). Philippe Francois Renault discovered this river in about 1720, and was struck by its beauty. He called it *Grande Riviere*, probably meaning beautiful or magnificent rather than large. The translation "big" for *grande* soon took over. It was called Renault's Fork of the Meramec for a while. Occasionally the river was referred to as Negro Creek, for reasons that remain unknown (RF).

Big Spring. There are 19 places called Big Spring in the state, including a town in Montgomery County (P.O. 1830-1906). However, the champion spring is in Carter County, at Big Spring State Park. An estimated 350,000,000 gallons a day roar from its basin into the Current River (LI).

Big Springs Country. This regional name for the counties in southeast Missouri west of the bootheel refer to the thousands of springs here. There are six categorized as "first magnitude," a reference to the U.S. Geological Survey scale defining springs in terms of water output. First magnitude springs have a flow greater than 100 cubic feet per second or 450 gallons per minute. See Big Spring.

Big Sugar Creek Country. This regional name for the counties around McDonald County refers to a grove of maples from which maple sugar and syrup was made. The sugar making gave the name to the creek. (LI).

Billings (Christian). Named for a Mr. Billings, he paid $1,000 to local churches for the honor (LI). P.O. 1870-now. Pop. 989.

Birch Tree (Shannon). This town is named for a landmark birch that stood by the early post office here (VR). P.O. unknown-1867, 1869-now. Pop. 599.

Bird's Blue Hole (Mississippi). This Department of Conservation lake is a "blue hole" created by man and nature during the flood of 1927. During the flood, several spots in the levee were blown up in agricultural areas. This relieved pressure from the levees that protected towns. The gushing water eroded a circular hole—called a "blue hole" or "blew hole"—in the flood plain (LI). Bird is a family name (RF). See Bird's Point.

Bird's Point (Mississippi). The first settlement in the county, this dates back to Spanish land grants. The river landing was bought by Abram Bird in 1805 and the place was named for him. On an old ledger kept by the warehouse and general store at Bird's Point the name is written in various ways. It appears as Bird's Landing, Illinois Point and Bird's Point (VR). P.O. 1886-1913.

Biscuit Rock (Texas). This huge rock looked like a biscuit, but it marked a dangerous spot for 19th- and early 20th-century rafters who floated lumber from the hills to markets on the Big Piney River. The rock is 12 miles north of Hazelton (GA).

Bismarck [BIZ mahrk] (St. Francois). This is named for the famous German statesman and founder of the German Empire, Otto Eduard Leopold,

Prince von Bismarck-Schonhausen (1815-1898). During World War I there was a movement by citizens to change the name of this town to Loyal (RF). P.O. 1868-now. Pop. 1,579.

Bit Nation (Clark). Back when hard money was scarce, Spanish coins brought from Santa Fe were cut into eight pieces and passed as currency. Each "bit" was worth 12.5 cents. Land in this part of the county was sold for one bit an acre (RF).

Black River. A tributary of the Mississippi River, this river was named for its color.

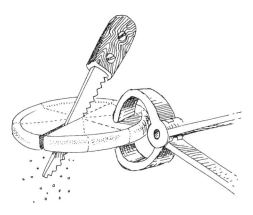

Blanchette Landing (St. Charles). Louis Blanchette, nicknamed "Le Chasseur" or "The Hunter," established a trading post at this spot in 1769 or 1770.

Blind Horse Bluff (Pulaski). When wild horses ranged the Ozarks in the free-range days, a blind horse fell off this bluff on the Big Piney River. It was killed when it struck the ground (GA).

Blind Pony Country (Saline). A local informant tells us he grew up here, and heard a lot of stories about the name. His favorite is about a pony that was used in the coal mines to pull coal carts. Some of the carts were so loaded that the ponies would "pull themselves blind" and the miners would have to destroy them. One was a particular pet of the miners, and they let it escape and run away one night.

"For years it roamed the area blindly grazing and feeding on what could be found to eat and drink from the old creek," our correspondent wrote. Occasionally, miners and farmers would bring it hay and grain. Eventually it disappeared. No one seems to know when or how it died, but our writer remembers riding back and forth to school on his own pony. He wondered when his pony "would act funny and spooky if it sensed the presence of another pony nearby off to the side of the road, in a timber or field somewhere maybe and I always felt that feeling too. That just may be that blind pony was there somewhere if only in spirit or in my mind" (LI).

Bloody Island. In the Mississippi River, opposite St. Louis, this heavily wooded island was the preferred site for settling disputes by duel. In 1822 and 1823, the practice had become so common that there was great public outcry and the custom was somewhat curtailed. Dueling continued until the 1830s and was finally outlawed (DM).

Bloomfield (Stoddard) county seat. This is the site of an ancient Indian village first settled by white people in 1824. The site was selected and the town laid out in 1835 by John McComb, Michael Rodney and Henry Shaner, who named the town for the large field of flowers they found there. P.O. 1836-now. Pop. 1,800.

Blue Eye (Stone). A dark-haired, blue-eyed Civil War veteran was the first postmaster here (LI). One local story tells that the postmaster had one blue eye and one brown (LI). P.O. 1870-1874, 1876-1883. Pop. 112.

Blue River. This river was named for the color of its water, especially as it was seen joining the muddy Missouri River (CG). In recent years, the name of this river has become ironic as the river flows through Kansas City and is a popular illegal dumping ground. In 1991, a Department of Conservation Stream Team of local volunteers carried out old tires, bedsprings, carpeting, part of a sofa, a refrigerator, two televisions, a water heater and a furnace (from <u>Missouri Conservationist</u>).

Bluffton (Montgomery). This town is laid out on a bluff above the Missouri River (CG). P.O. 1867-1966.

Boeuf Creek [BEF] or [BUHF] (Franklin). *Boeuf* is French, meaning "cow," "ox" or "buffalo." The creek was probably named for buffalo. The town had two names: Detmold was a village name before the post office was established; people continued to use it even after the post office was named Boeuf Creek (RF). P.O. 1857-1915.

Boiling Spring (Texas) A settler built a dam on a branch of the Big Piney, which was intended to create a millpond. After a particularly heavy rain, the pond and the stream mysteriously disappeared. A few miles down the creek, a new spring boiled out of the ground. They concluded the pond had caved in and emerged as this new spring. The term "boiling" describes the force of the water rising from the ground—not its temperature. Known for its beauty and size, it was also reputed to be an excellent fishing hole (LI).

Bois d'arc [BOH dark] (Greene). This town was named for an impressive bois d'arc hedge planted by an early settler (RF). P.O. 1868-now.

Bolivar [BAH luh vuhr] (Polk) county seat. This town was named by settlers for the county seat of Hardeman County, Tennessee. Tennessee's Bolivar was named for Simon Bolivar, the patriot who freed Peru from the Spanish (RF). In Missouri, a statue of Simon Bolivar the liberator stands in a town park. P.O. 1836-now. Pop. 6,845.

Bollinger County [BOH ling (g)uhr] or [BAH lin juhr]. In 1796, Colonel George Frederick Bollinger settled on Whitewater River. He became acquainted with the commandant of the post at Cape Girardeau, who promised him land if he would bring more settlers to the district. Bollinger went to North Carolina and returned with his wife and twenty colonists and families, all of German or Swiss parentage and members of the German Reformed Church (RF). Organized 1851. Pop. 10,619.

Bon Ton Bend. This bend in the Missouri River was named by early French settlers. The name means "Good Town" in the sense of well-mannered (CG).

Bonanza (Caldwell). This town was renowned for its vigorous spring, which had a lot to do with its existence. The town was named by a Dr. Smith for the Spanish word associated with unexpected, lucky prosperity (RF). P.O. 1881-1903.

Bonhomme Creek [BAH nuhm]. Named by neighbors for Joseph Herbert, a settler who was particularly easy-going, honest and popular. *Bon homme* is French for "good man." First called *La Riviere au Bonhomme*, the road to his house was called Bonhomme Road (CG).

Bonne Femme Creek [bahn FAM]. The name is one of the oldest French names in the state, and its origin is a matter for speculation. The words mean "good woman," but why streams in Randolph and Callaway Counties were so called is a mystery. Perhaps the names honor the Osage, whose leader was known as Good Man, and his wife, Good Woman. Meriwether Lewis translated the names to Goodwoman's Creek and River, but the old French prevailed. A legend to explain the name tells of a pioneer's wife named Famie, and a starving Indian who asked for "A bone, Famie" (RF).

Bonne Terre

Bonne Terre: The Ramsay File

Bonne Terre [bahn TER] (St. Francois). The name of this early French settlement means "good earth." It was given by miners to clay ground containing lead, to distinguish it from the worthless clay ground adjacent (APM). The spelling has varied: Bontear, Bonneterre, and in 1906, it changed to its present form. The settlement was also known as the St. Joe mines, probably for St. Joseph, husband of Virgin Mary, who was thought a patron saint of miners. Today, the flooded lead mine is used for recreation by scuba divers. P.O. 1868-now. Pop. 3,871.

The Ramsay File

A state treasure, the Robert Ramsay place name file at Western Historical Manuscript Collection in Columbia should be the first stop for anyone interested in the subject. Amassed between 1928 and 1945, the file contains place name stories from every county collected by masters degree students of English professor Robert Ramsay at the University. The file is composed of 3x5 cards each recording the story of the name of a waterway, geographical feature, town, railroad landmark, school, church, road, or other place. There are almost 35,000 cards, and the quality varies greatly.

Ramsay estimated that "it is quite possible to make at least six mistakes in discussing any single place name: that is, in its spelling, its pronunciation, its location, its date, its name-father, and in the exact circumstances of its invention or adoption," yet he believed that correct answers existed. He passed on his systematic methods to students, who read all the sources they could find about their counties, interviewed people they knew, and wrote down the stories.

If there was a golden age for place name study in Missouri, it was the years of Ramsay's tenure. Besides the file, he left us books including Our Storehouse of Missouri Place Names (University of Missouri Press.) Name lovers should have this in their collections.

The file lives on, fifty years later, as an authority, a friend and an entertainment. We have been working with the Ramsay file for years. We know how frustrating it is for someone who knows a really good—really true—story about a place name and discovers something completely different in the file. Who is right—the story teller of today or the story teller of yesterday? Like many questions in history, this is what makes life interesting.

Bonnot's Mill [BAH nahts MIL] (Osage). The town was laid out by Felix Bonnot, and his mills gave the place its name. Also known as Dauphine, for the wife of the heir to the French crown (LI). P.O. 1857-1869, 1892-now. Pop. 190.

Boone County [BOON].. Boone County was named in honor of Daniel Boone, the pioneer and Indian fighter. He died about two months before the county was formed, and members of the legislature were wearing badges of mourning in respect to his memory (RF). By the time Missouri officially became a state, Boone County had been organized for almost nine months and the Smithton Land Company was doing a land-office business selling lots at the county seat. In their haste to choose a site for the county seat, Smithton stockholders failed to ensure the area had an adequate water supply. In May 1821, Smithton was abandoned for a site near Flat Branch Creek, and the town of Columbia was platted around a cabin on what is now the southeast corner of Broadway and Fifth Street. Organized 1820. Pop. 112,379.

Boone's Lick (Howard). In 1808, Daniel Boone's sons Nathan and Daniel, who had come into the country in 1807, distilled salt from the water of the salt springs they found here. Salt was needed for food seasoning and preservation, leather tanning and many other things. The salty spring was called a "lick" because animals gathered there to lick the rocks. See also Boon's Lick Country.

Boon's Lick Country. The region takes its name from the Boone saltworks. Local historian Bob Dyer defines this region as "west of Cedar Creek and north and west of the Osage River . . . the present day counties of Boone, Howard, Saline, Cooper, Moniteau, and Cole bordering the Missouri River." See Boone's Lick and Boonslick Trail.

Boonsboro (Howard).. Named for the sons of Daniel Boone. See also Boone's Lick. P.O. 1871-1953. Pop. 50.

Boonslick Trail. The path from St. Louis to Boone's Lick. Part of it follows Interstate 70. This name is also written Boone's Lick and Boon's Lick Trail.

Boonville (Cooper). Named for the sons of Daniel Boone. See also Boone's Lick. P.O. (estimated) 1825-now. Pop. 7,095. See also Fort Cole.

Daniel Boone

The Kentucky exploits of Daniel Boone are well known, but in his later years, the bluegrass state became too crowded for the heavily indebted, restless entrepreneur and he headed for Missouri. Promised Spanish grants and honors, he settled on a farm of 1,000 arpents (845 acres) in St. Charles County. The Spanish government still controlled Missouri country and encouraged Americans to cross the Mississippi and establish permanent settlements.

Boone was appointed chief officer to the Femme Osage area in June of 1800. His duties included justice of the peace and militia commandant. Barely literate, he wrote about his duties:

I am hire With my hands full of Bisness
and No athoraty, and if I am Not indulged in
What I Do for the best it Is Not worth my While
to put my Self to all this trubel...

Boone lived his last days in the Missouri homes of his two sons, leaving frequently to hunt and trap to continue paying off his debts. He was often called upon to settle disputes, and the "judgment tree" where he listened to arguments and dispensed wisdom is still standing in Defiance.

Daniel's sons, Daniel Morgan Boone and Nathan Boone, had better luck in business than their father. They developed salt licks in Howard County, processing the salt from spring water and shipping it east to St. Louis along an overland trail north of the Missouri River that became known as the Boone's Lick Trail. Over the years, Boone's Lick became Boonslick, and the region acquired the nickname "The Boonslick." Several towns along the trails acquired similar names, including Boonsboro and Boonville.

As with other legendary figures, it is sometimes hard to separate fact from fiction in the accounts of Daniel's life. A favorite story recounts that artist Chester Harding visited the fearless Boone to paint his picture. He found Boone roasting a venison steak on a ramrod. In their conversation, Harding asked Boone if he had every been lost in the wilderness. "I never was lost," Boone is supposed to have replied, "but I was bewildered once for three days."

Boone was supposed to be afraid of nothing, even death. Ever prepared, he stored his coffin under his bed. Every now and then, dressed his best, he climbed in, checking it for size and proving he was prepared to face the Grim Reaper. These naps may have been the most peaceful moments he spent therein, as after death Boone's remains were the subject of dispute between Missouri and Kentucky. After he died in 1820, he was buried near Marthasville beside the grave of his wife. A slave was also buried in the small family plot.

In 1845, Kentuckians petitioned to remove Boone and his wife to a plot overlooking their capitol. Boone, who swore he'd never set foot in Kentucky again, was supposedly removed.

True Missourians, however, and several historians, believe that only his wife and slave were displaced. If this is true, the lonely Boone slumbers in his original grave.

Bootheel
Braggadocio

Bootheel. Yes, it looks like a bootheel. In 1818, John Hardeman Walker learned that Missouri's southern border would match up with the southern borders of Kentucky and Virginia at 36 degrees, 30'. This would have left Walker's land in the wilderness. After surviving Indian wars and the New Madrid earthquakes, he saw statehood as protection. He campaigned that land between the Mississippi and St. Francis Rivers to the 36th parallel be included in the new state. He won (VR).

Bourbeuse River [BUR bus]. This name is a very early French one; *bourbeuse* meant "muddy, miry, sloshy, sloughy." In its upper length, the river is comparatively clear; the name fits better the lower part in Franklin County. Other spellings have been Bourbois, Bourboise, Burbois, Burbus (RF).

Bourbon (Crawford). (1) This town was named for the whiskey, which was a new flavor in the mid-1800s. The storekeepers bought a quantity and their success was assured (APM). (2) Probably named for Bourbon County, Kentucky, which was named in Revolutionary times for the royal family in France (GS). P.O. 1853-now. Pop. 1,188.

Bowling Green (Pike) county seat. This was named by its first Kentucky settlers after Bowling Green, Kentucky, and laid out on the same plan (RF). P.O. 1820-1821, 1824-now. Pop. 2,976.

Braggadocio [BRAG uh doh shuh] (Pemiscot). There are lots of stories about it: (1) Maybe the first settler had a beautiful wife named Docio and he bragged about her all the time (RF). (2) The more likely source is Edmund Spenser's book The Faerie Queen, today the bane of M.A. candidates in English literature. This book was part

The sleepy Ozark town of Branson became a tourist center when it was discovered by country singing stars and their fans.

APRIL 8, 2009

of the standard library of the eighth-grade-educated pioneer. One of Spenser's comic heroes was a boastful knight and horse thief named Braggadocchio, with "flowing tongue," "puffed up with smoke of vanity" (RF). The word *brag* used as an adjective meaning "favorite" was common in pioneer days; folks spoke of their "brag hound," "brag pupil," etc. (LI). P.O. 1881-now. Pop. 450.

Branson (Taney). This was named for R.S. Branson, the town's first postmaster. In 1902 the name was changed to Lucia because of a dislike for a Branson descendent, but in 1908 it was changed back (RF). This town has become a center for country-and-western theaters, and is said to attract the second highest number of visitors of any tourist site in the United States (Disney World is first) (LI). P.O. 1882-now. Pop. 3,706.

Branson West (Taney). Located near two lakes, this town was named Lakeview until 1992. After the great success of Branson, Lakeview changed its name to Branson West. Pop. 37.

Brown County. In 1872, residents of Johnson, Lafayette, Pettis and Saline Counties proposed a new county around the town of Brownsville (Saline), now called Sweet Springs. The proposal failed. See also Sweet Springs.

Brunswick (Chariton). This river town was laid out in 1836, one mile below the mouth of Grand River. It was named by the Reverend James Keyte for his former English home, Brunswick Terrace (CG). The town's future as a shipping point dimmed as the railroad bypassed it to the north, then as the Civil War brought ruin.

Finally, in 1875, the river changed course and left Brunswick a mile inland (VR). Today, it is the state's center for pecan growing and processing. Brunswick is also home to the world's largest pecan, weighing 12,000 pounds (LI). P.O. 1836-now. Pop. 1,074.

Bryant River. This is named for a hunter and trapper by the name of Bryant who settled on the river about 1830.

Buchanan County [byoo KAN uhn]. First known as Roberts County, it was renamed in honor of James Buchanan of Pennsylvania. An American idol, he afterwards became president of the United States (RF). Organized 1839. Pop. 83,083.

Bucksnort Creek
Bushwhacker Wildlife Area

Bucksnort Creek. A salt lick here was the gathering place for deer during mating season. Their snorting could be heard far off, so the place was named Bucksnort.

Bucyrus [byoo SEYE ruhs] (Texas). This village was first called Odd (P.O. 1892-1898), by Ransom Lynch, a leading citizen. Postal authorities were not amused and asked for a change. Someone chose the name of the town in Ohio which was either (1) the birthplace of the postmaster's wife (APM), or (2) Lynch himself (RF). P.O. 1898-now.

Buffalo (Dallas) county seat. This name is in dispute: It may have come with settlers from Buffalo, New York (RF). That city, in turn, may have gotten its name when the English tried to pronounce the French *Beau fleuve*, or "beautiful river," referring to the Niagara River (LI). Or Buffalo, New York, may have been named for an Indian who lived nearby (GS). An alternative idea: The area around the Missouri town was known as Buffalo Head Prairie. It was named when a group of hunters found a buffalo skull and put it on a stick as a landmark for others (Enc). P.O. (Polk) 1840-1842, (Niangua) 1842-1846, (Dallas) 1846-now. Pop. 2,414.

Bull Creek (Christian). This creek was named by hunters after they killed four buffalo calves here one morning (LI).

Burch (Wayne). This was first called Exist, an example of pioneer humor in a place where people could barely make it. The name was changed when landowner Burch founded a post office in his home (RF).

Bushwhacker Wildlife Area (Vernon). This name was selected by the Department of Conservation to commemorate the troubles of that area during the Civil War (LI).

Butler County [BUHT luhr]. Named for the honorable William Orlando Butler of Kentucky, who was very popular with southern democrats and was the (unsuccessful) democratic candidate for vice president in 1848. Organized 1849. Pop. 38,765.

Buttsville (Grundy). Named for its first postmaster, this tiny manufacturing town was developed by a woman. A weaver and spinner, she began a textile cottage industry. The town is remembered as close-knit. Later, coonskin caps and deerskin moccasins became part of the trade (LI). P.O. 1855-1902.

Cabins, The (Adair). This region, also called Cabins of White Folks, six miles west of Kirksville, was the first white settlement in the county. When members of the Iowa Nation visited and insulted the women, settlers retaliated. This was one of the incidents that touched off the Black Hawk War (APM).

Cabool [kuh BOOL] (Texas). This railroad town was named by real estate developers for the market capital of Afghanistan. According to some locals, however, the town was named after a Native American chief who fell in love with and kidnapped the daughter of the Chief Pomona. When the father brought his braves to free her, Cabool and the maiden plunged to their deaths over a cliff rather than be separated (RF). P.O. 1882-now. Pop. 2,006.

Caldwell County [KAWLD wel]. General Alexander M. Doniphan named this county in honor of Matthew Caldwell, commander of Indian Scouts in Kentucky. General Doniphan's father, Joseph Doniphan, had belonged to Captain Caldwell's Indian Scouts and had often spoken of Captain Caldwell as a brave and gallant soldier (RF). Organized 1836. Pop. 8,380.

California (Moniteau) county seat. Although it would seem that this town was named during the California Gold Rush, it was named for a man— California Wilson. At the raising of the logs of the first buildings, he offered to treat the party with two gallons of whiskey if the boys would name the town after him (LI). P.O. 1845-now. Pop. 3,465.

California Trail, The. In the late 1840s, gold was discovered in California and thousands of Missouri men went west. Wagon trains to Oregon and prospectors to California traveled through the Rocky Mountains together then split apart. Some went northwest to Oregon and others west to California. See Yolo.

Callao [KAL ee oh] (Macon). The first postmaster, seeking a name for the village, put his finger on a map of South America and found it pointing to Callao, Peru (VR). P.O. 1859-now. Pop. 332.

Callaway County [KAL uh way]. Captain James Callaway, grandson of Daniel Boone was one of the leading men of his time in the state. He met his death March 8, 1815, in Montgomery County, where he had led an attack on the Sacs and Foxes who had stolen some horses from the settlers (LI). Organized 1820. Pop. 32,809.

Calumet [KAL yu met] (Pike). This short-lived town was named for the creek. P.O. 1872-1907.

Calumet Creek. The French called peace pipes *chalumeau*, or "reeds." This was Americanized to Calumet (JL). The calumet was used principally in the Mississippi River valley (RF).

Camden County [KAM duhn]. Originally named Kinderhook, for Kinderhook, N.Y., home of Democratic Martin VanBuren. VanBuren abandoned the Democratic party in 1848, and the horrified county scrambled to change its name. The new name honors Charles Pratt, Earl of Camden, an English politician who supported the young colonies in the Revolutionary War (RF). Organized 1841. Pop. 27,495.

Camdenton (Camden) county seat. "Camdenton is NEW and UNIQUE" boasts a 1931 motor club manual. "It has been laid out along approved lines by expert city planners" (KM). Nicknamed for its location at the crossroads of State Hwy 5 and U.S. Highway 54, "the hub city of the Ozarks" was named for its county. P.O. 1931-now. Pop. 2,561.

Cameron (Clinton-DeKalb). This town was named for Colonel Elisha Cameron, father-in-law of Samuel McCorkle, one of the town's founders (VR). P.O. 1855-now. Pop. 4,831.

Campbell's Landing. This landing on the Missouri River was famous among boatmen for its buttermilk, and was also called Buttermilk Landing. Steamboats would sound a special signal to call for it. Mr. Campbell, proprietor, could point out from his hill thirteen places where steamboats had gone down (BH).

Cane Creek
Carondelet

Cane Creek or **Caney Creek**. Creeks in Bollinger, Butler, Cape Girardeau, Carter, Dunklin, Howell, Scott and Taney Counties are named for the plants that grew on their banks. Cane was helpful to early settlers who used large canes for fishing rods, fencing and plant supports. The small cane could be used for pipe stems for corn-cob and clay pipes.

Canton [KAN tn] (Lewis). Named for the town in Ohio, an order of Druids organized here. Their principles were founded on reason and sound morality. Like other Druids, Canton Grove No. 36 performed their rites in oak groves (RF). P.O. 1835, 1847-now. Pop. 2,623.

Cape Fair (Stone). This name may be an Americanization of a Delaware tribe name, but some locals insist that the name was Cape Fear, given by pioneers as they looked back at the steep ridges they climbed in their covered wagons (LI). P.O. 1847-1858, 1878-1879, 1886-1887, 1889-now.

Cape Girardeau [KAYP juh RAH doh] or [KAYP juh RAH duh]. Cape Girardeau county seat. A trader named Girardeau or Girardat traded here at Cape Rock as early as 1760, but there were no houses for 30 years. Finally, a few settlers came to live here and named their new town after him (RF).The nickname "City of Roses" refers to a test garden; some of the rose bushes came with settlers from England before the founding of America. See Cape Girardeau County. P.O. 1806-now. Pop. 34,475.

Cape Girardeau County. The county name was taken from the settlement. This was one of the first five counties organized when Missouri was still under territorial government. Organized 1812. Pop. 61,633.

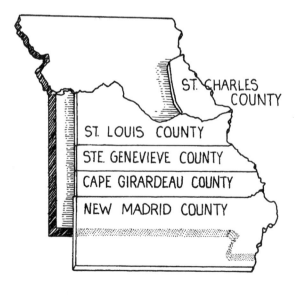

Carondelet [kuh RAHN duh let]. This settlement was first known as Delor's Village, for the first settler. Then it was renamed Catalan's Prairie, for another early French inhabitant. Later it was named Louisbourg, probably for the King of France. The present name, which is the name of the Spanish governor who took over Louisiana Territory in the years of Spanish control, was given by a French official. He gave the name to flatter the Spanish governor and thereby keep his position (RF). See also "Vide Poche." P.O. 1826-1873.

Carroll County [KAIR uhl]. The name intended for the county was Wakenda but at the time of the county's organization, the news of the death of Charles Carroll reached Jefferson City. He was a Revolutionary War hero and signer of the Declaration of Independence (RF). Organized 1833. Pop. 10,748.

Carrollton (Carroll) county seat. After its organization, the county was granted 80 acres, and chose the highest point therein for its courthouse (MO). It was named for Carrollton Manor, the Maryland estate of Charles Carroll (CG). See also Carroll County. P.O. 1834-now. Pop. 4,406.

Carter County [KAHR tuhr]. This county was named for the first settler, Zimri A. Carter. In a beautiful part of the state, it is the home of Big Spring State Park, one of Missouri's first state parks. Organized 1859. Pop. 5,515.

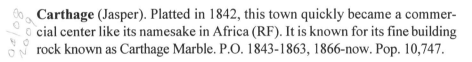

Carthage (Jasper). Platted in 1842, this town quickly became a commercial center like its namesake in Africa (RF). It is known for its fine building rock known as Carthage Marble. P.O. 1843-1863, 1866-now. Pop. 10,747.

Caruthersville [kuh RUH dhuhrz vil] (Pemiscot) county seat. The first settlement in this area was La Petite Prairie, named by French traders who also referred to East Prairie, Long Prairie and Big Prairie. The name was Americanized to Little Prairie. The settlement was destroyed by the earthquake of 1811-1812. Caruthersville was laid out a few miles north and was named for Sam Caruthers of Madison County, a congressman (RF). P.O. 1856-1864, 1866-now. Pop. 7,389.

Carver School. There are dozens of Missouri schools named for George Washington Carver, the world-famous scientist who was born a slave. Most were built for African American children, and many were dedicated by Carver himself. The names of other successful African Americans were used for all-black schools during segregation days. Frederick Douglass and Paul Lawrence Dunbar each are honored with school names.

Cass County
Catalpa Park

Cass County [KAS]. First named Van Buren County, for Martin VanBuren, the county changed its name after the 1848 election. The Free-Soil party nominated VanBuren for president, splitting the Democratic vote between VanBuren and Democratic nominee General Lewis Cass. Because of the split, Whig Zachary Taylor was elected. The General Assembly of Missouri was so discouraged that they voted to change the name of Van Buren County to Cass (RF). Cass County was so plundered during the Civil War that it was called The Burned District. Organized 1835. Pop. 63,808.

Cassville (Barry) county seat. Named for Lewis Cass (see Cass County), this city was the site where Confederate and home guard forces gathered before the Battle of Wilson Creek in 1861. More than 10,000 pro-southern soldiers met here, leaving the town with the nickname "Confederate Capital of Missouri in 1861." It was destroyed by the Union Army after the Battle of Pea Ridge. P.O. 1845-now. Pop. 2,371.

Catalpa Park (Barton). G.H. Walser (see Liberal) became a spiritualist and established this place to worship, in a beautiful grove of catalpa trees.

Carthage marble has been used for buildings all over the United States, including Missouri's state capital.

Catawissa [KAT uh wis uh] (Franklin). Platted by the Frisco Railroad in 1858, the town borrowed its name from a Pennsylvania town. Two theories: *Catawissa* is the Conoy Indian word meaning "growing fat" (RF). Or, Algonquin *piscatawese* means "place of white pines," a name of the Conoy tribe (JL). P.O. 1860-now. Pop. 170.

Catfish Chute. Riverboat men named this shallow stretch of the Missouri River between Washington and St. Louis for the often seen fish.

Cedar City (Callaway). As early as 1825 there was a post office located here called Hibernia. Cedar City was laid out in 1866 by David Kinney. In 1870 the town incorporated. The Chicago and Alton railroad line from Mexico, Missouri, arrived in 1872 and terminated here. Passengers got off the train and a horse trolley took them to the ferry to cross the river to Jefferson City. In the 1890s, a toll bridge was built. Cedar City was all but washed away by the flood of 1993. In fact, its name already seems relegated to history, as it has been annexed to Jefferson City and many people from the area refer to it as North Jefferson (BD). P.O. 1870-now.

Cedar County [SEE duhr]. This county was named for Cedar Creek, which was named by Lewis and Clark because of the cedars along its bank (CG). The first public building in Missouri to be made of poured concrete is the Stockton courthouse, dedicated in 1940 (MO). Organized 1845. Pop. 12,093.

Centertown (Cole). This was first called Lookout because there was a nearby railroad signal proclaiming "Look out for the cars" (RF). The name was changed because founders believed their town was in the geographical center of the state (Enc). P.O. 1893-1894. Pop. 356.

Centerville (Reynolds) county seat. Probably named for its location in the county, some residents say it was named because of a large sycamore tree that stood in the center of town (RF). P.O. 1892-now. Pop. 200.

Centralia [sen TRAYL yuh] (Boone). This town occupies a central position on the old North Missouri line from Ottumwa, Iowa, to St. Louis; it is also in the center of a vast prairie bordered roughly by the towns of Mexico, Huntsville, Paris and Columbia (RF). Here, Bloody Bill Anderson and 350 Confederate guerrillas invaded the town, stopped a train and slaughtered arriving Federal soldiers. To avenge this, a force of 175 Union men came to Centralia but they were also killed (VR). P.O. 1858-now. Pop. 3,414.

Centropolis (Kansas City). This town was roughly between Kansas City and Independence, and named in a uniquely American way, was by putting the Greek *-opolis* onto the Latin *centro-* (RF).

Chadwick (Christian). When John Chadwick, a railroad foreman, was kicked in the head by a mule and died, an official told his men to bury him in the next town, which was no more than a few log cabins. The town thus became named. P.O. 1883-now.

Chain of Rocks (Lincoln). The town on the north side of the Cuivre River was named for a series of exposed limestone rocks on the bluff. P.O. 1869-1907.

Chamois [shuh MOI] (Osage). The bluffs overlooking the river reminded settler Morgan Harper of his native Switzerland. He named the town after the small, goatlike antelope native to the alpine region (RF). P.O. 1856-now. Pop. 449.

Charrette Creek [SHAIR uht] or [shuh RET]. The French name, which means "Cart Creek," may come from the homemade carts used by French settlers who farmed these bottoms. Another source suggests the name is a corruption of the name of a French fur trader who drowned here (CG).

Chariton County [SHAIR uh tuhn]. This was named after a river in the county. See Chariton River. Organized 1820. Pop. 9,202.

Chariton River. A corruption of the name "Thieraton" for John Thieraton, an early explorer and fur trader, the name appears in many forms—Charleton, Charlaton and Charlotte, for example (CG). The river is a tributary of the Missouri River.

Charleston (Mississippi) county seat. Two opinions: (1) Families from the South developed cotton plantations in the lowlands here and named this city after the city in South Carolina (VR). (2) The town was named for Charles Moore, who granted the land and helped develop it (RF). P.O. 1892-now. Pop. 5,085.

Chillicothe [chil uh KAH thi] (Livingston). This town was named for Chillicothe, Ohio; it is Shawnee for "Big town where we live" (VR). P.O. 1839-now. Pop. 8,804.

Chinquapin (McDonald). In Algonquin, this may mean "Great fruit or seed," an appropriate name for the giant oak found many places in Missouri (JL). The word, also spelled chinkapin, has been used to designate a dwarf chestnut tree, but more commonly refers to the oak or its acorn (LI).

(Christian) County [KRIS chuhn]. This county was named at the request of an old lady who had lived in the Kentucky county by that name (RF). It served as one of the home bases for the Baldknobbers, a vigilante citizens' group sworn to bring justice to horse thieves and other criminals. Organized 1859. Pop. 32,644.

Clarence (Shelby). This was probably named for Clarence Duff, a child of the principal contractor for building the St. Joseph Railroad. P.O. 1859-now. Pop. 1,026.

Clark County [KLAHRK]. Named for William Clark, one of the leaders of the Lewis and Clark expedition that followed the Missouri River to the Pacific Ocean. This expedition, called together by President Thomas Jefferson, was to report on the newly purchased Louisiana Territory west of the Mississippi. See also Lewis County. Organized 1818; reorganized 1836. Pop. 7,547.

Clarksville (Pike). In the 1850s, the orchards around the town gave it the name Appletown, though it was probably better known for its "snaking frolics." In one day, it was said, a hunting party killed 700 rattlesnakes. Another boasted of killing 9,000. The snakes are mostly gone now and the town was renamed in honor of Governor William Clark, who is said to have camped here one winter (VR). P.O. 1819-now. Pop. 480.

Clay County [KLAY]. Henry Clay, a brilliant orator and popular senator from Kentucky, was beloved by Missourians struggling to maintain their southern identity (RF). In 1824, Clay ran for president. He was defeated nationally, but won in Missouri, thanks partly to the efforts of orator Thomas Hart Benton (DM). See also Ashland. Organized 1822. Pop. 153,411.

Claysville (Boone). When the river port shipping town of Stonesport was washed away in 1844, the residents moved back from the river. This new town was named Claysville. When the MK&T railroad was built in 1892 closer to Hartsburg, businesses migrated there. Only a few structures remain.

Clayton
Clover Bottom

Clayton (St. Louis) county seat. Ralph Clayton, a citizen, donated 100 acres of his farm for the new county seat (RF). P.O. 1885-1901, 1904-1913. Pop. 13,874.

Clear Branch (Morgan). *Branch* is another word for *creek*, but not to the highway department. Their sign renames it Clear Branch Creek (LI).

Clearwater (Ste. Genevieve). Named by the first postmaster in 1930 for the town in Florida where his cousin lived. Clearwater is a "stock" name; it was used in Wayne County earlier, and is found in 11 states altogether. P.O. 1929-1981. Pop. 50.

Clever [KLEV uhr] (Christian). This little town was named by a founder because "clever people lived there." *Clever* means not only intelligent, but kind and good-hearted (RF). In a reversal of the usual waterway-to-town naming pattern, Clever Creek is named after the town. Pop. 580.

Climax Springs (Camden). The self-glorifying name Climax is a stock name; it is found in American towns in nine states (RF). The "Springs" was added in 1886 when a group of businessmen started promoting the "fizz water" of a nearby spring. Visitors came to cure scrofula, syphilis, rheumatism, epilepsy, "female diseases" and other maladies (LI). P.O. 1883-now. Pop. 91.

Clinton [KLIN tn] (Henry) county seat. A 1922 publication calls this a "progressive and well-governed little city with a population of 5,000—and every one a live wire." The town was named for DeWitt Clinton (see Clinton County). For a few years in the late 1800s, Clinton was home to Baird College for Women, which encouraged thrift. "Extravagance in youth leads to poverty in old age" says its manual. P.O. 1850-now. Pop. 8,703.

Clinton County. The popular DeWitt Clinton, a governor of New York and prime mover in constructing the Erie Canal, was honored by this county name. When the site for the county seat was determined, an opportunity-seeking county judge rushed to the land office and put the parcel in his name, then offered to sell to the county at a profit. The county foiled his plan and relocated the seat of justice slightly to the east (LI). Organized 1833. Pop. 16,595.

Clover Bottom (Franklin). Jesuit missionaries were amazed by the fields of clover, which they took as a sign of rich soil. Early settlers joined them, mostly from Poland and Germany. P.O. 1869-1920s.

Cole Camp [KOHL] (Benton). The Coles of Cooper County had camped on the creek here, watering stock, hunting and exploring (APM). See also Fort Cole and Cole County.

Cole County. This county was carved out of Howard County and was named for Stephen Cole, a pioneer settler. The Howard county seat was located at Cole's fort. See also Fort Cole and Cole Camp. Organized 1820. Pop. 63,579.

Collinsville (Butler). Three Collins families lived near this station on the Ruth and Hargrove Tram Railroad (RF).

Columbia [kuh LUHM bi yuh] (Boone) county seat. There are at least two versions of how Columbia got its name. (1) The name demonstrates the new county's patriotic attachment to "Columbia, the gem of the ocean" or "for the queen of the world and the child of the skies" (RF). (2) Another, more likely version, is that Columbia was settled largely by former Kentuckians who brought the name of Columbia, Kentucky, with them. Legend has it that in 1840 young Abe Lincoln courted Mary Todd here. Mark Twain received an honorary doctorate at MU, and the Rolling Stones brought their Voodoo Lounge concert tour here in 1994. P.O. 1821-now. Pop. 69,101.

Commerce (Scott). According to locals, there was a trading post here as early as 1803, date of the Louisiana Purchase. The name was given because of the town's commercial nature (LI). P.O. 1834-now. Pop. 173.

Conception (Nodaway). Named for the Basilica of the Immaculate Conception, visitors here are amazed to find a Romanesque cathedral and monastery in the middle of cornfields.

Conception Junction (Nodaway). Near Conception, this town sprang up where the Wabash and Chicago Railroads crossed (RF). P.O. 1864-1865, 1868-now. Pop. 236.

Confusion (Montgomery). This is a post office name suggested by a postmaster who had submitted, and seen rejected, a long list of possibilities. The post office required that names be distinctive (RF). P.O. 1891-1893.

Congo
Crawford County

Congo (Shannon). This post office was named by a resident interested in geography. He had been studying the rivers of Africa (RF). P.O. 1895-1931.

Contrary Creek. Before the Corps of Engineers constructed a drainage canal that empties this creek into the Missouri River, it ran parallel to the river, and in the opposite direction (CG).

Cooper County [KUP uhr]. Sarshell Cooper was killed when he was shot by an Indian through a hole in the wall of his fort. He had a child on his lap when he was shot. The child was uninjured (RF). Organized 1818. Pop. 14,835.

Cooter [KOO tuhr] (Pemiscot). By 1856, this was a flourishing hunting and fishing camp with a special abundance of coots, a member of the duck family. Occasionally through the years the name has been spelled Couter, and the post office even tried to change it to Coutre to avoid confusion with Cooper in Gentry County. This changed spelling leads some to say the place was named after an early French settler, Portell Coutre from New Madrid (RF). P.O. 1882-now. Pop. 451.

Cote Sans Dessein (Callaway). In Mississippi River French, *cote* was usually applied to a line of hills along a waterway. Usually, this place name is taken to mean "hills without design," or "misshapen hills." P.O. 1818-1825, 1826-1829, 1838-1876, 1882-1907.

Courtois Creek [KOH tuh way]. Probably named for a French settler, Americans misspelled and repronounced this name until it sounded like and was occasionally written Cotoway or Coataway (RF).

Cowskin River. This is an old name for Elk River, with at least two explanatory stories. In one, an early settler lost a herd of cows—30 or 40—to a mysterious ailment near the river. In an attempt to make something of his loss, he skinned them all and left the skins to dry on the banks (RF). The skin and tallow was the most valuable part of a cow (CG). Another story dates the name somewhat earlier to a Catholic priest who named the river after a buffalo cow was killed and its skin made into a robe (RF).

Crawford County [KRAW fuhrd]. This was named for Georgian William Harris Crawford (1772-1834). In 1824, he was nominated Democratic candidate for president. There being a tie, the decision was made in the House of Representatives, which finally chose the Whig candidate John Quincy Adams (RF). Pop. 19,173.

Creve Coeur [KREHV kor] (St. Louis). The lake and town are named in French "Broken Heart" not for a sad tale about a broken-hearted maiden, but after a fort in Illinois. The fort, in turn, was named by Robert de LaSalle in 1689 to honor a military victory in France (RF). P.O. 1851-1959. Pop. 12,304.

Crooked River. This waterway was first called Big Creek because of its size. It was renamed because of its shape (CG).

Cross Roads. This was a common name for a town appearing where two roads came together or crossed. Here, farmers would find places to take care of everyday needs—a general store, a church, a school, a blacksmith and a mill where corn and wheat could be ground. In the late 1800s, the post office began delivery to many rural places. To have a post office, a town had to have a name unlike any other in the state, so crossroad towns scrambled for new names. "Cross Roads" was claimed by three Missouri post offices at different times: Gasconade 1840-1847, St. Francois 1858-1862, Douglas 1909-1959.

Cross Timbers (Hickory). This name originated from the name of a settler called Cross who built a log cabin in the vicinity, surrounded by timber (LI). The term was used in early days for a belt of forestland (RF). P.O. 1847-now. Pop. 168.

Crowder State Park
Cynthianna Creek

Crowder State Park. This park is named to honor Missourian General Enoch Crowder, who designed the selective service system.

Crystal City (Jefferson). This town was founded to manufacture glass. The plate glass made here, starting in 1872, was called by Walt Whitman "the clearest and largest, best, and most finished and luxurious in the world" (VR). P.O. 1872-now. Pop. 4,088.

Cuba (Crawford). After they spent a holiday on this island, two gold miners brought the name back to this railroad town in the Ozarks (VR). P.O. 1860-now. Pop. 2,537.

Cuivre River [KWIV uhr]. From the French *Riviere au Cuivre*, meaning "River of copper," perhaps because the earliest French believed there was copper in the stream (VR). Other opinions are that the river's name came from its copper color after a flood or that it was explored by French Barron de Cuvier, a naturalist (RF).

Cureall [KYOOR awl] (Howell). This was originally a resort with several springs said to cure various ailments. At one time, the hotel and bathhouse were a popular tourist destination; the town boasted several homes, a saw mill, grist mill, stores and post office (RF).

Current River [KUHR uhnt]. This tributary of the Mississippi River is fed by seven clear, cold springs. It is named for the French word *courant*, which means "swift-running water." The river falls seven feet per mile (VR). The name may go back to Spanish *corriente* (RF).

Cyclone (McDonald). In 1880, a great cyclone passed through this part of the state. This post office, founded three years later, was named in its honor (RF).

Cynthianna Creek. According to legend, a beautiful girl tried to drown herself here when she was disappointed in love. She did not succeed; the creek is too shallow (CG).

D

Dade County [DAYD]. The county was named for Francis L. Dade, a Virginian, who became a lieutenant, captain, and brevet-major in the U.S. Army. He was killed in a fight with the Seminole tribe in 1835, near Fort King, Florida (RF). Organized 1841. Pop. 7,449.

Dadeville (Dade). A post office named Crisp Prairie, in honor of an early pioneer, was joined by a mill, ensuring the success of the place. Three citizens were given the chance to draw straws to name it. The winner, a Dr. Hampton, selected the name Mellville. After discovery that mail was being missent to Millville, the name was changed to that of the county. P.O. 1858-now. Pop. 220.

Daisy (Cape Girardeau). This new name was given to Drum Town when it applied for post office status. There are conflicting stories: (1) The local doctor suggested that the name be given for a baby he had just delivered; (2) a town wag suggested the name of a woman of ill repute in the area (LI); (3) it was named for the wife of an old settler in the county (RF). P.O. 1887-now. Pop. 70.

Dallas County [DAL uhs]. First named Niangua, for the river that winds down its eastern border, citizens changed the name because Niangua was "too hard to spell and pronounce." It adopted the name of the new vice president George Mifflin Dallas (1792-1864) (RF). Organized 1844. Pop. 12,646.

Damascus (St. Clair). Originally named Cross Roads, the name was changed to that of the Syrian market town, probably because of its Biblical connection (RF). P.O. 1895-1906.

Dangerous Branch. This short stream is unprotected by trees, so it is subject to winds, currents and sudden rises (CG). The word *branch* is a synonym for *stream* (LI).

Danville
Defiance

Danville (Montgomery). One of many Missouri towns settled by southerners, this was named for Danville, Virginia (LI). It was selected in 1834 as the seat of Montgomery County. On October 14, 1864, Bloody Bill Anderson and 80 of his guerrillas galloped into the village, shooting residents they thought were southern sympathizers and burning down most of the buildings including those containing the county records. The town never recovered (VR). P.O. 1834-1942. Pop. 75.

Dardenne Creek [DAHR duhn] (St. Charles). This name may be a corruption of *Terre d'Inde*, French for "the land of turkeys," a plentiful game bird in those parts (APM).

Darien [DAIR ee uhn] (Dent). This is a literary name, reminding us that the early settlers valued their traditional education. It comes from a line by Keats: "Silent, upon a peak in Darien." (RF). P.O. 1888-1954.

Daviess County [DAY vis]. This county was named in honor of Colonel Joseph H. Daviess who died in the battle of Tippecanoe, on November 7, 1811 (RF). In early days, this county was home to a large settlement of Mormon families, and the site of a massacre of Mormons. Organized 1836. Pop. 7,865.

Davisville (Crawford). First called Boyd, for the grist mill owner, the town was known for a long time as Pucky-Huddle. The name was given by an Irish man, who remarked on the huddle of people at the saloon. The Irish *puca* is an elf or sprite, and derivatives like *pixy*, or *puckish* mean "devilish," "wicked" or "mischievous." The town was later named for the Davis family who ran the post office, 1880-now (RF).

Dearborn (Platte). This town was named for General Henry Dearborn, a Revolutionary War soldier and secretary of war under Thomas Jefferson. P.O. 1883-now. Pop. 480.

Deepwater (Henry). On the earliest maps of the county, the creek is named Deepwater. The town picked up the name from the creek (LI). P.O. 1885-now. Pop. 441.

Defiance (St. Charles). (1) When Harve Matson started promoting his nearby town of Matson to the detriment of this settlement, people here became angry. One of the citizens named this town as a comment on the mood (VR). (2) Early settlers in the Defiance area were of English extraction, from either Virginia or Kentucky. James Craig, aware of the significance of the railroad to small towns, led a crusade of volunteers to build a depot and a farm-to-market road (now Defiance Road). The town was then named Defiance because it had lured the railroad away from Matson in 1893 (BD). The Schiermeier store here sports two opposite-facing fronts. One front faces the railroad, while the other front faces the farmers and local agriculture. P.O. 1893-now. Pop. 200.

DeKalb County [dee KALB]. Part of the Platte Purchase, this county was named in honor of Baron John De Kalb, a Frenchman who fell in the battle of Camden in 1780 (RF). Pop. 9,967.

Delaware. Several southwest Missouri towns and one Department of Conservation area bear the name of this Native American nation that originally inhabited the eastern seaboard. They called themselves "Lenape" (real men). When their land was taken by the English in 1789, they were invited to move to Missouri by the Spanish government (LI).

Demeter (Camden). Named for the goddess of fruitful soil and agriculture, this town only lasted a few years. P.O. 1898-1908.

Dent County [DENT]. This county was named in honor of Lewis Dent, a Tennesseean, who was the county's first representative in the Missouri general assembly. Organized 1851. Pop. 13,700.

Des Arc [DEZ ahrk] (Iron). Two ideas: (1) The railroad makes a curve (or arc) here, to go around a hill (RF). (2) Like Ozark, this name reminds us that the Arkansas Indians (Arks) once lived here (GS). P.O. 1871-now. Pop. 173.

Des Peres [duh PAIR] (Saint Louis). The official name for this settlement of French missionaries and Kaskaskia Native Americans was St. Francis Xavier; it was nicknamed *"des peres,"* French for "the Fathers." A very early settlement (1700), it was soon abandoned and resettled much later as Highway City. The name was changed back in 1876. P.O. 1848-1902. Pop. 8,395.

De Soto [dee SOH to] (Jefferson). Called Nopton after the founder's friend, and judge of the Missouri Supreme Court; the name was changed to honor

Deslet
Devil's Elbow

Hernando DeSoto. The local library reports fielding many queries from folks who believe the town was founded by the explorer, but not so (LI). It is nicknamed "The Fountain City" because of its many artesian wells (Enc). Many states have Mississippi River towns named for the explorer who discovered the river (GS). P.O. 1858-now. Pop. 5,993.

Deslet [DES let] (Shannon). Deslet was so desolate that it was so named. The namer made a spelling mistake. P.O. 1896-1955.

Desloge [duh LOHZH] (Saint Francois). Named for Firmin Desloge, developer of an important lead company here and pioneer of the Lead Belt (LI). P.O. 1892-1963. Pop. 4,150.

Devil's. Much of our state is undergirded by a cave system that contributes to the topography with limestone arches and ridges, openings into the earth's chilly interior and hundreds of springs. Because these come from underground, and even may smell of sulphur, it is natural that the pioneer place namer gave the Devil his due. There are over a hundred "devil" names in the Ozarks alone.

Devil's Backbone. This stock name is given to ridges in Jackson, Phelps, Ripley and Oregon Counties, and a rough road in Montgomery.

Devil's Boot Cave (Warren). This rock cave looks like a boot, with a top entrance about 25 feet across and a leg about 30 feet deep. Perhaps the Devil stepped in here, leaving the impression of his boot (RF).

Devil's Den (Webster). This unusual sinkhole, mostly filled with water, was thought bottomless because weighted measurement devices never seemed to touch down (KM).

Devil's Elbow (Butler). In Missouri, the Devil has several elbows, including this dangerous bend in Black River, several miles south of Poplar Bluff.

Devil's Elbow (Pulaski). About 35 miles north of Hazelton, this is a bend in the Big Piney River where numerous log rafts met their demise. U.S. Highway 66 (now U.S. Highway 44) crosses the Big Piney at this place (GA). There is a town here. P.O. 1927-now. Pop. 300.

Devil's Icebox (Boone). This sinkhole is the entry to a cave. A part of Rock Bridge State Park, naturally cool air is present at the entrance even in hottest weather.

Devil's Icebox (Madison). Climbing to the top of 600-foot-tall Pilot Knob for a picnic is a special treat. At the top, hikers are refreshed with a blast of cool air from the entrance to a cave.

Devil's Race Ground (Franklin). This half-mile of Missouri River was renowned for its treacherous swiftness (RF).

Devil's Run Creek. This small creek in Carter County is renowned for its swiftness and also for the rough characters who lived thereabouts (RF).

Devil's Toll Gate (Iron). A passage about 8 feet wide, 50 feet long and 30 feet high through a rocky section of Taum Sauk Mountain, the road that passes through was a passage on the Trail of Tears.

Devil's Wash Basins (Warren). Three washed-out basins in the rock give this place its name (RF).

Devil's Washpan (Lawrence). The site of a resort, this spring resembles an old-fashioned washpan (KM).

Devil's Well (Shannon). This natural well is about 100 feet deep, fed by an underground stream (KM).

Dewey Bald Knob (Taney). This 1,341-foot peak is mentioned in the popular novel Shepherd of the Hills (VR). Bald mountains are so named because of their lack of trees on the top. This one was named Dewey for an old miner who spent his life there searching for gold after the California gold rush of 1849 (RF). A town once existed by the name. P.O. 1916-1933.

DeWitt (Carroll). Its name reflects its tempestuous history: First called Eppler's Landing for a settler, the first official name was Elderport. In 1837 it was changed to DeWitt, then briefly in 1851 to Windsor City for a developer, then back to DeWitt. Once an important riverboat town, DeWitt was the scene of Saturday "law day" when complainers, defenders, lawyers and spectators came to town to air their differences. Occasionally, due process broke down and disputes settled by melee (CG). Pop. 125.

DeWitt County
Doe Run Creek

DeWitt County. This was a "phantom" county that only succeeded in developing one town, Waynesville. It became part of Pulaski County.

Dexter (Stoddard). Named for a racehorse owned by a Mr. Dex, this town was also called Dexter City (Enc). See also Lewis County. P.O. 1873-now. Pop. 7,559.

Diamond (Newton). Near the birthplace of George Washington Carver, the town was known as Diamond Grove for the diamond-shaped stand of walnut trees. Today, the George Washington Carver Monument commemorates the life and work of that scientist and conservationist (VR). P.O. 1883-now. Pop. 775.

Dickens (Taney). This town was named for the beloved English writer, Charles Dickens. P.O. 1899-1958.

Diehlstadt [DEEL stat] (Scott). "Diehl's town" in English, this name provides an excellent example of what happens to ethnicity when a name is tossed into the melting pot of America. Named for a German settler, H.J. Deihl, the settler-storekeeper's name was misspelled Deal by a signpainter. Deihl kept the new spelling, but the town did not. Later, during World War II when anti-German sentiment was high, there was an unsuccessful movement to change the name to Liberty (RF). Pop. 145.

Dixie (Callaway). This name is always associated with the South, and came to Missouri with southern Americans. Its roots are obscure. The most likely theory is that it came from the French *dix* meaning "ten," printed on banknotes from a bank in New Orleans. They became known as dixies (GS).

Dodd's Island. This island, the largest in the Osage River, was owned by James Dodd, boat owner. Dodd's three sons were born here; all became famous boatmen (BH).

Dodge County. This county is now part of Iowa. See Unionville.

Doe Run Creek (Reynolds). Settlers found that this was a path for the deer in the country. Later, the name was adopted by a town in St. Francois County and a large lead-mining company, which still operates here (RF).

Dog Creek (Daviess). See Marrowbone Creek.

Dog Creek (Miller). A tributary of the Osage, this creek was named to mark a spot where a hunter was attacked by a dog (RF).

Dog Hollow (Barry). Before the Civil War, this name was given to a hollow southeast of Purdy for the many dogs belonging to foxhunters that lived there (RF).

Dog Hollow (McDonald). Local informants say this place was named for the dogs that hunted there (RF).

Dog Patch. Of all place names given for animals, the number of dog names leads the pack. We know of at least three settlements called Dog Patch in Missouri. The name just fits a place where dogs outnumber people, and also refers to the hillbilly settlement of the comic strip "Li'l Abner."

Dog Prairie (St. Charles). This prairie was called Prairie du Chien by Lewis and Clark for the prairie dogs or kit foxes found here. *Chien* means "dog," and prairie dogs were called *petit chien*, or "little dog." Another mammal, the kit fox was known as *chien de prairie*. Other names for this place have been White's Prairie in honor of the first settler here, and Comegris' Prairie in honor of the first miller here. Those who have forgotten Lewis and Clark say that Dog Prairie may have gotten its name to celebrate a big dogfight that took place at the mill, but the Lewis and Clark reference is probably the true first name (RF).

Dog Town (Harrison). Several Missouri settlements have had this name because of the many dogs that lived therein. Harrison County's was named for the first law case in the county court. The plaintiff charged the defendant with killing his dog (RF). (For another famous dog law case, see Warrensburg.)

Dog Town (St. Louis City). Perhaps named because it became the residence of packs of dogs released after the St. Louis Louisiana Exposition in 1904. In a celebrated court case, authorities won the right to supply the Fair's resident Philippine community with Humane Society dogs, which were cooked and eaten in the Philippine village. When the Fair ended, the Philippinos stayed on, settling briefly in Dog Town with their dogs. They didn't stay long. St. Louis winters proved too cold (LI).

Dog Town (Texas). Seven miles north of Hazelton on the Big Piney, large packs of stray dogs roamed around here, fighting men and each other (GA). The name has been remembered with the Missouri Department of Conservation's Dog Bluff Access.

Dog Trot (Dunklin). A boggy part of the county where only the dogs knew where to find solid ground and were light enough to trot across (LI).

Dogtown (Dallas). See March (Dallas).

Doniphan [DAH nuh fuhn] (Ripley) county seat. Alexander Doniphan was a famed Missouri soldier who led troops during the Mexican War. His name was used for a post office in Grundy County (1847-1848). When it went out of business, the name was appropriated by this town. Missouri supplied more troops to that war than any other state, which explains the many Mexican names appearing here (VR). P.O. 1848-now. Pop. 1,713.

Douglas County [DUHG luhs]. Named for Stephen A. Douglas, at the height of his popularity (RF). Douglas suggested that the new Territory of Kansas should be a slave state, settled mostly by Missourians. To balance, Nebraska, settled by Iowans, would be a free state. Organized 1857. Pop. 11,876.

Douglass School. There are at least eight Missouri schools named for Frederick Douglass, a slave who became a famous leader, writer and speaker. These were built for African American populations.

Dresden (Perry). This short-lived community was one of five in Perry County founded by Germans. It was probably named for the capital of Saxony, home of their founding pastor (RF). See Altenburg.

Dresden (Pettis). This German name is so commonly used in the United States that it is considered a stock name. In Germany, the town is known for its delicate and elaborately decorated porcelain figures (RF). P.O. 1863-1954. Pop. 200.

Duden's Hill (Warren). Named for Gottfried Duden, who wrote <u>Report on a Journey to the Western States of North America</u>, a book describing the wonders and beauty of Missouri. As a result of Duden's work, thousands of German settlers emigrated.

Dumpville (Pettis). This town was named not for its atmosphere or major industry but for a resident, Peter Dump, who lived there. P.O. 1884-1905.

Dunklin County [DUNG klin]. The county was named for Honorable Daniel Dunklin, governor of Missouri 1832-1836. He surveyed the boundaries of Missouri and Arkansas, and it is probably because of this connection that the county was named for him (RF). One of his interests as governor was to establish public schools (DM). Pop. 33,112.

Dutzow [DUHT zoh] or [DOOT zow] (Warren). Founded by the Berlin Emigration Society in 1832 (VR), this is an early German settlement, named by a wealthy landowner after his estate near the Baltic Sea in Germany. The streets were named for German poets. Here settlers could perpetuate their customs, handicrafts and hillside agriculture undisturbed by the tensions and strife that plagued the German states in the 19th century. In 1839, Jesuit priests came regularly to Dutzow, or Duseau as it was then called. Soon a parish was established and the first Saint Vincent de Paul Church was built in 1842. The railroad came through in the 1890s and the town prospered. P.O. 1869-now.

Eaglette
Eaudevie

E

Eaglette (Stoddard). Many places in Missouri are named for the majestic eagle, and the name endured even as eagle populations disappeared. Eagles are being re-established and once again raise their young (eaglets) in the cypress swamps and river lands (LI).

East Lynne (Cass). This name is for a romantic novel by Mrs. Henry Wood about rural life. The novel was translated into dozens of languages and dramatic versions were performed by traveling groups all over the United States (RF). P.O. 1871-now.

Eaudevie [OH duh vee] (Christian). Medicinal water from springs here was shipped to distant states until it was found there were no special qualities to it (APM). The name, *eau de vie*, is French for "water of life." It was given by promoters. P.O. 1880-1930.

Economy (Macon). C.H. Nelson, the founder, adopted the motto, "It is economy to buy at this place." P.O. 1856-1906.

"Eden." Charles Dickens used this name to describe the almost nonexistent frontier town of Marion City (Marion). See Marion City.

"Eden of Louisiana." The ballad Evangeline was published by Henry Wadsworth Longfellow in 1866. A sentimental love story about a young and faithful Acadian heroine in pursuit of her lost true love, part of the action takes place in Missouri where, the poet intones, "They who dwell there have named it the 'Eden of Louisiana.'" Wadsworth's "Eden" is described as rich and beautiful, inhabited by innocent adventurers and helpful Native Americans.

Charles Dickens' "Eden"

The English novelist Charles Dickens visited the United States and came by steamship to Missouri in 1842. In Dickens' 1843 novel, Martin Chuzzlewit, the author depicts a fledgling architect and his manservant who travel to America to find fortune. The hapless pair are set upon by New York promoters and taken to a land office, where they see a map of the deliciously named Eden:

"Heyday!" cried Martin, as his eye rested on a great plan which occupied one whole side of the office . . . "Heyday! what's that?"
"That's Eden," said Scadder . . .
"Why, I had no idea it was a city."
"Hadn't you? Oh, it's a city."
A flourishing city, too! An architectural city! There were banks, churches, cathedrals, market-places, factories, hotels, stores, mansions, wharves; an exchange, a theatre; public buildings of all kinds, down to the office of the Eden Stinger, a daily journal; all faithfully depicted in the view before them.
"Dear me! It's really a most important place!" cried Martin, turning round. *continued*

JULY 20, 2008

Eden:
Excerpt from Charles Dickens

"Eden"
continued

"Oh! it's very important," observed the agent.

"But, I am afraid," said Martin, glancing again at the Public Buildings, "that there's nothing left for me to do."

"Well! it ain't all built," replied the agent. "Not quite."

When the heroes arrive in Eden, which Dickens modeled after the frontier village of Marion City, Missouri, they find that "The waters of the Deluge might have left it but a week before: so choked with slime and matted growth was the hideous swamp which bore that name . . . " Most of the population had left, or died, and those who remained were ill with an unnamed fever. The few cabins were mostly abandoned and wrecked, the air was bad, the citizens living in fear of raids from wild animals and Indians. Still, the lads hung their shingle "with as much gravity as if the thriving city of Eden had a real existence, and they expected to be overwhelmed with business."

Finally, the luckless fellows are sent money to return to England. Much relieved and much wiser, they depart with a final salute. Martin's unfailingly cheerful companion observes that if he was to paint a portrait of the American Eagle he would: "draw it like a Bat, for its short-sightedness; like a Bantam, for its bragging; like a Magpie, for its honesty; like a Peacock, for its vanity; like an Ostrich, for its putting its head in the mud, and thinking nobody sees it—"

"And like a Phoenix, for its power of springing from the ashes of its faults and vices, and soaring up anew into the sky!" said Martin. "Well . . . Let us hope so."

JULY 20, 2008

Eden City (Dent). This name was given hopefully for the Biblical garden where Adam and Eve, first humans, lived in innocent bliss.

Edgewood (Pike). This town was located on the edge of a rough patch of timber. P.O. 1879-1955. Pop. 35.

Edina [ee DEYE nuh] (Knox) county seat. Named by Stephen Carnegie, a surveyor and a Scotsman from Edinburgh, Scotland. He had surveyed a town he called Edinburg in Scotland County, and to this new town he gave the name Edina, the Scottish city's ancient name and classic title (RF). P.O. 1850-now. Pop. 1,283.

Egypt (Ray). After a flood, one of the early settlers returned home by raft. When he returned, he remarked that he was "going back to Egypt," comparing the fertile soil to that of the Nile Valley.

El Dorado Springs (Cedar). According to one story, a St. Louis woman traveling to Hot Springs, Arkansas, for her health was forced to stop here to rest. After two weeks of rest and water from the local springs, she was well enough to return home. Entrepreneurs wasted no time in publicizing the case, and, within five years, a resort town was thriving on the spot (Enc). Meaning "The Golden" or "Gilded Land," this is a stock name; fourteen other cities in the United States are named Eldorado (RF). The post office name has been changed, wavering between Eldorado Springs (1894-1940) and El Dorado Springs (1881-1894, 1940-now). Pop. 3,830.

Eldon (Miller). The name Elmira, for the wife of an early settler, was first given to this town, but the popular name was rejected because it was already in use. Eldon was the name of a surveyor for the railroad (RF). P.O. 1881-now. Pop. 4,419.

Eldridge (LaClede). This settlement was originally peopled by freed African Americans after the Civil War. Their leader was Alfred Eldridge. After the turn of the century, most of the inhabitants migrated to the cities (LI). P.O. 1886-now.

Electric Place (Saint Francois). This town, occasionally called Power House, was served by the electric railway (RF).

Electric Spring (Johnson). When it had a chance to be a tourist town, Colbern's Spring looked for a modern name. Electricity was thought to have special healing powers (RF).

Elephant Rocks State Park (Iron). These large, granite rocks have long been a local wonder and attraction. The name comes from their size. They probably were rectangular when broken away from the mass, centuries ago, but have been weathered away into rounded shapes (VR).

Eleven Point River [uh LEV n] or [uh LEB m] (Oregon). This name is an old one, probably going back to the earliest French voyageurs. *Points*, in Mississippi Valley French, were wooded arms of land that protruded into the stream. Modern explanations of the name include the story that a buck was shot here with an unusually large rack of antlers, and the story that surveyors found the stream so crooked they had to change the points of their compass eleven times as they followed it (RF).

Elk Creek (Texas). Elk were uncommon in Missouri, but were occasionally seen. A few waterways and settlements bear their names. P.O. 1860-1863, 1869-now. Pop. 60.

Ella Ewing Lake (Scotland). One of the smallest lakes owned by the Department of Conservation, this was named for a local lady who reached the height of 8'4". She earned her living by exhibiting herself with traveling shows, then came home to retire in a specially built house. Even though her height was not documented well enough to earn her a place in the <u>Guiness Book of World Records</u>, neighbors and fellow Missourians have never doubted it.

Elvins (St. Francois). Named Setz for a local landowner, the post office changed to Elvins for Jesse Elvins, another landowner (RF).

Eminence [EM uh nuhns] (Shannon) county seat. The original pre-Civil War town stood on a bluff with its courthouse overlooking the Current River. The new Eminence is in a hollow because, some say, the first wagon carrying materials for a new courthouse broke down at the foot of the hill and inhabitants were too lazy to repair it. The new courthouse and town are 40 miles away from the old (RF). P.O. 1844-now. Pop. 582.

Enon [EE nuhn] (Franklin, Moniteau, Saint Charles). (1) Local surveyors named these places when they could not find any outstanding features about the place. When there was nothing significant, they named a place "none" spelled backwards. (2) A simplified form of Aenon, a river mentioned in the New Testament: "John was also baptizing in Aenon . . . because there was much water there" (GS).

Enough [EE nuhf] (Iron). After a post office applicant had sent two hundred names for approval, he finally called his town "Enough." P.O. 1916-1937.

Eolia [ee OHL yuh] (Pike). By tradition, this town was named on a very windy day; the name comes from Aeolus, Greek god of winds (GS). P.O. 1881-now. Pop. 389.

Esther (St. Francois). Briefly called Columbia, for the Columbia Lead Mines, the town was renamed, probably for a daughter of a lead company owner (RF).

Ethlyn [ETH luhn] (Lincoln). This railroad stop was named for the teenaged daughter of the local store owner. She was a favorite of the railroad men who stayed there (LI).

Etlah (Franklin). This is the place where a group of German immigrants stopped and settled. In German, *halte* (the town named spelled backward) means "stop" (GS). P.O. 1864-1935.

Eureka (Jefferson). The surveying engineer of the Missouri Pacific Railroad may have named this town when he discovered that a route through this valley would eliminate many steep cuts and grades (RF). "Eureka!" is an expression of delighted discovery, usually having to do with a financial windfall. (There was also a short-lived Eureka in Boone County, from 1854-1858.) P.O. 1860-now. Pop. 4,683.

Everton (Dade). When the railroad came through, all the houses from nearby Cross Roads and the hotel from Corry were moved to this site. There had been a post office, Rock Prairie, here but it had moved from house to house, serving only a few people (APM). With the new population, the town was renamed for a Mr. Evert or Everett. P.O. 1881-now. Pop. 325.

Evona (Gentry). This post office has the distinction of spelling its name backwards for a time. From 1880-1905 and 1925-1935, it was Evona. From 1916-1925, it was Anove. Other names for the evasive community were Albany and Bone Set (LI). P.O. Evona 1880-1905, Anove 1916-1925, Evona 1925-1935.

Ewing (Lewis). This trading center was originally called Bestville, for the superintendent of the Quincy, Omaha and Kansas City Railroad, then Briscoe Station for a local family. When the post office was established, the name was changed to that of an early resident. P.O. 1894-now. Pop. 463.

Excelsior (Morgan). Two ideas: The name comes from a poem by the popular 19th-century poet Henry Wadsworth Longfellow (VR); the Excelsior Wheel improved mill machinery in the 1850s, perhaps the name came from this wheel (RF). At any rate, *excelsior* is a Latin word meaning "upward"; it has served as the motto of New York and is a popular ideal name for towns and schools all over the United States. P.O. 1866-1922.

Excelsior Springs (Clay). One of the first health spas in Missouri, this resort became popular after 1880 when fishermen found water with a mineral taste. The nearby town, Viginti, changed its name to promote the waters, which were thought to cure rheumatism, tuberculosis and other sicknesses. Soon, railroad lines from Kansas City and Chicago came to Excelsior Springs, bringing tourists to fancy hotels, baths and swimming pools. After the first spring (Old Simon) was developed, others followed: Saratoga, the Relief and the Empire (VR). The Art Deco Hall of Waters was built in 1937. P.O. 1883-now. Pop. 10,354.

Exeter [EXS uh tuhr] (Barry). This town is on the highest hill in four counties (Newton, Lawrence, Barry and McDonald) (APM). The name is associated with excellence (LI). P.O. 1880-now. Pop. 597.

F

Fabius Junction [FAB ee uhs] (Marion). This post office at the junctions of the North Fabius River and South Fabius River took its name from the rivers. P.O. 1876-1877, 1879-1887.

Fabius River. This many-branched river bears one of the oldest names in North Missouri; its origin is still mysterious. It is referred to on maps as Fabiane, Fabba, Fabin's. There is some agreement that the present name was taken from Roman General Fabius Maximus; this makes it fit with classical names Hannibal, Palmyra and Scipio also appearing in northeast Missouri. It may even have been the first of these classical names, and suggested by the name of a French trader. A disregarded theory: It was a name given by the Spanish for a bean that grew in the vicinity (RF). See Hannibal, North River. P.O. (Scotland) 1876-1878, (Schuyler) 1879, (Knox) 1897-1935.

Fagus [FAY guhs] (Butler). Named by a classics lover, this is Latin for "beech tree." (GS). See Quercus. P.O. 1913-1973.

Fairdealing (Ripley). A traveler awoke after spending the night here and found that his horse had been stolen but his saddle was left. "Well, now, that's fair dealing," he is reported to say (LI). Another story tells that a traveler traded a saddle here, and felt he got a fair deal (APM). Still another places the story during the Civil War and focuses on the thief, "a rough fellow," who stole a fine horse but left the saddle (APM). P.O. 1883-1886, 1895-now. From 1886-1895, the post office name was spelled with two words: Fair Dealing.

Fairview. This name has been used by many Missouri towns, including (at different times) four post offices. Officially, it has been in use in 30 states. The post office department finally called a halt to its use (APM). Pop. 298.

Farmington
Fiddlers Ford

Farmington (St. Francois) county seat. This was known as Murphy Settlement during the last years of the Spanish regime (Enc). It takes its name from its location in the richest farming section of the county; there are Farmingtons in 25 other states, making this a stock name (RF). P.O. 1825-now. Pop. 11,598.

Fayette [FAY et] or [fay ET] (Howard) county seat. This town was founded and named after news reached the area that French revolutionary hero Lafayette was to visit America. He did not visit his namesake, but he did enjoy a hero's welcome in St. Louis. P.O. 1824-now. Pop. 2,888.

Fee Fee Creek (St. Louis). This odd name is an Americanization of a French nickname, *fi fi*, similar to "sonny" in English. The "sonny" was one of the first settlers in St. Louis, Ferdinand R. Nicholas Beaugenou. A post office took the name from 1842-1859.

Femme Osage [FEM oh SAYJ] (St. Charles). This is a very old name, given by the French for an Osage woman or princess, perhaps the wife of a chief. *Femme* is French for "woman." P.O. 1816-1818, 1828-1833, 1839-1908.

Fenton (St. Louis). The town was named for Elizabeth Fenton Long, wife of a prominent man.

Festus (Jefferson). Famous for its taverns, this village was first named Tanglefoot, perhaps to honor its patrons as they walked home. In 1878, when the town was finally platted, the founders sought a respectable name. They opened the Bible and saw, "Then Agrippa said unto Festus, I would also hear the man myself . . . " and read no further (VR). P.O. 1883-now.

Fiddlers Ford (Dade). A public land, this was named for a reference on old topographical maps. The fiddler was a main source of entertainment in the community; fiddles and fiddle traditions were passed from generation to generation, and can be traced back to European set-

tlers. The fiddle was named Missouri's official state instrument in 1987. Also, a fiddler was a type of young catfish with a forked tail; some rivermen believed it was a distinct species of fish altogether (LI).

Fifteen Springs. See Seven Springs.

Fillmore (Andrew). This town was named for Millard Fillmore, who was becoming a major political force. He was elected president in 1850 (RF). P.O. 1857-now.

Firth (Randolph). This settlement was first named Milton for the North Carolina hometown of a founder; the name was changed because Milton was in use in Atchison County. The new name was that of a Moberly postmaster (RF). However, Firth never had a post office (LI).

Fish Trap Shoal (Pulaski). The old rafters put their fish traps out here, about 23 miles north of Hazelton on the Big Piney River (GA). To the Ozarker, *shoal* is a verb meaning "to assemble for breeding or spawning," as fish and suckers do; occasionally, it was also used to describe the sinful gatherings of young people (RF).

Fishing River (Ray). This was a popular fishing spot for Kansas Citians (RF). P.O. 1821-unknown.

Five Cent Hill (Washington). When lead and tiff were dug here, the yields were small (RF). APRIL 22, 2009

Five Points (New Madrid). This small switch was named by the Frisco and Cottonbelt Railroads because lines branched in five directions: Northeast, southeast, northwest, southwest and south (RF).

Flat Creek (Barry). Sources disagree on the origin of this name. Is it a corruption of the French *platte,* which means "shallow" or "flat"? Does it describe the flat terrain? Does it describe flat rocks at the bottom of the creek (RF)? The creek spawned a town; the post office wrote the town name as two words 1840-1845, 1855-1863 and 1865-1894, then one word 1894-1923.

Flat River (St. Francois). This is a descriptively named flat and shallow stream that eventually empties into descriptively named Big River (RF).

Florida
Fort Cole

The river spawned a town, which recently merged with others to form Park Hills. See Park Hills. P.O. 1867-1876 (estimated), 1886-1994. Pop. 4,823.

Florida (Monroe). Samuel Clemens (Mark Twain) remembered his birthplace as a town of two streets "paved with the same material: tough mud in wet times, deep dust in dry" (VR). The two-room log cabin where he was born is preserved inside a modern museum. P.O. 1832-1968.

Florissant [FLOH ruh suhnt] (St. Louis). This town was called St. Ferdinand by Spanish authorities but Florissant, which is French for "flowering," by its French residents. It was known as St. Ferdinand de Florissant until 1939 when the name was officially shortened (VR). Eighth in population, the city sponsors an annual Valley of Flowers festival featuring Maypole dancing, tours of historic homes, contests and a beer garden. P.O. 1818-1901, 1904-now. Pop. 51,206.

Fordland (Webster). A local trader started a black walnut and pecan exchange here in 1931, and the area quickly became the state's fruit, nut and berry center. The town is named for a railroad official named J.S. Ford (LI). P.O. 1882-now. Pop. 523.

Foristell [FAW ris tel] (St. Charles). Originally called Snow Hill, this post office changed its name to honor a wealthy farmer and cattle dealer (LI). P.O. Snow Hill 1859-1873, Foristell 1873-now. Pop. 144.

Forsyth [FOR seyeth] (Taney) county seat. Named for John Forsyth of Georgia; he was secretary of state and an outstanding figure in the Democratic party. The town was once the headquarters of the Baldknobbers, an organization formed July 4, 1884, on the summit of one of the bare-topped hills. The young vigilantes sought out criminals at first, then turned against tie hackers, squatters and homesteaders who moved onto free range (LI). P.O. 1837-1863, 1866-now. Pop. 1,175.

Fort Clark (Jackson). This fort, later called Fort Osage, then Fort Sibley, was built in 1808 on a site first noted by Lewis and Clark in 1804.

Fort Cole (Howard). Occasionally called Fort Hannah or Cole's Fort, this fort was named for Hannah Cole. In 1807, the Cole family was traveling to Boone's Lick. They were attacked by Sauk Indians who stole their horses and killed Hannah's husband. She went on with her nine children and one cow, arrived at a place near present-day Boonville, built her cabin, and planted corn. The first year the family diet was mostly wild game, acorns and slippery elm bark. There were still Indian attacks and in 1814, the settlers built a stockade fence of logs with openings for a rifle barrel. After peace came, the fort served as a community center, courthouse, voting place, schoolhouse, church, post office and hospital (Source: Mary K. Dains, ed., Show Me Missouri Women. Kirksville: Thomas Jefferson University Press, 1989.)

Fort Osage. See Sibley.

Fort Zumwalt State Park. This 45-acre park is maintained around the remains of Jacob Zumwalt's home, a 1798 fort (LI).

Frankenstein (Osage). Not named for the monster, this town was probably named for Gottfried Franken, an early settler. There is also a Frankenstein in Germany. P.O. 1893-1921.

Franklin [FRANG klin] (Howard). The start of the Santa Fe Trail, this town was named for Benjamin Franklin (see also Franklin County). Early wagon trains to Santa Fe were put together here, then crossed the river on the ferry at Arrow Rock, then to Fort Osage and to a western trail. Franklin was flooded in 1827 and rebuilt farther from the river as New Franklin

New Franklin is where the Santa Fe Trail began. New Franklin is also "where the four trails meet" because the Santa Fe Trail, the Boonslick Trail, the Katy Trail and the Lewis and Clark Trail all pass through town.

Franklin County
Fremont

(LI). It was here in 1819 that the Missouri Intelligencer and Boonslick Advertiser, the first newspaper west of St. Louis, began. That same year, the riverboat *Independence*, which was the first steamboat to successfully navigate the Missouri River, docked in Franklin. It was the Santa Fe trail opening in 1821 that marked the beginning of the settlement of the Missouri River Valley as well as the admission of Missouri to the Union as a state (BD). P.O. 1821-1892, 1900-now. Pop. 181.

Franklin County. Named in honor of Benjamin Franklin (1706-1790), he was a Philadelphia printer, inventor, philosopher, diplomat, statesman, and one of the founders of our country. There are at least 20 Franklin Counties in the United States, and over 50 other towns and cities named for him (RF). Pop. 80,603.

Fredericktown (Madison) county seat. The first settlement here was Saint Michael, a French village. Across the Saline River, Germans settled with groups of American southerners. Soon, they outnumbered the French. Fredericktown gradually absorbed St. Michael. Two ideas about the name: It was possibly named for George Frederick Bollinger, a North Carolinian (see Bollinger County). A perhaps better explanation is that it was named for Frederick Bates, a German (see Bates County). P.O. 1827-now. Pop. 3,950.

Fredonia [FREE dohn yuh] (Ray). This town was platted just after the Civil War, as a town for newly freed slaves. It never really took off, however. The place name was popular in the 1800s and was suggested as a name for the United States itself. It was made up by a New Yorker who said it meant a land "of the free privileges and doings" (RF). It was used by post offices in St. Francois County 1866-1868 and Benton 1895-1910.

Freeburg (Osage). The original name was Engelbert, then Frankberg for the first postmaster, Engelbert Franke. The name was translated to English when Mr. Franke retired. *Franke* means "free" in English, and *berg* is spelled burg (LI). When the Rock Island Railroad was planned to pass through town in 1902, the future of this community seemed assured. The railroad, however, did not pass through town; engineers found it more economical to tunnel 997 feet through the ridge and go under the town than to grade the ridge down (VR). P.O. 1893-now. Pop. 446.

Fremont (Carter). Early Fremonts were probably named for John C. Fremont, explorer and Civil War general also known as "The Pathfinder" for directing an army unit through unknown territory during the Mexican War. Fremont lost favor for his actions in the Civil War and the present-day town is probably named for founder A.J. Freeman (GS). P.O. (Cedar) 1847-1859, (Clark) 1874-1884, (Carter) 1907-now.

Frieden Gemeinde [FREE dn guh MEYEN duh] (St. Charles). This means "community of peace" in German.

Friedheim [FREED heyem](Cape Girardeau). Named by the Germans, this means "home of peace." (GS).

Friendly Prairie (Pettis). This cheerful prairie name was given by the Missouri Department of Conservation to balance the melancholy name of nearby Hi Lonesome Prairie.

Friendship (Caldwell). This tiny Mormon community hopefully chose an ideal name. P.O. 1878-1883.

Frisbee (Dunklin). It is sometimes said that this was a Spanish name, given by the French. According to this theory, the French gave Spanish names to places they didn't like (LI). More likely, the name was that of a railroad official. P.O. 1907-1908.

Frohna [FROH nuh] (Perry). One of five Perry County communities founded by the earliest German Lutherans in Missouri, this was first known as Nieder-Frohna, in Germany the home parish of most of the settlers. The name was probably shortened because some of the settlers came from the adjoining Mittelfrohna (RF). See Altenburg. P.O. 1870-now. Pop. 246.

Fulton (Callaway) county seat. This town was first named Volney for Count Constantin Volney, French scientist and atheist. Volney's Ruins was a popular book with American readers, and at least a dozen American towns were named for him. Two months later, a resident named Bob went from door to door lobbying for a name change. Fulton (for Robert Fulton, who built the first steamboat) was deemed a better name (VR), even though the town was a day's overland travel from any water large enough to float a steamboat. For years, town dwellers used the nickname Bob (LI). P.O. 1825-now. Pop. 10,033.

G

Gainesville (Ozark) county seat. This town was named for Gainesville, Georgia, because many residents were from that area (RF). P.O. 1860-1863, 1867-now. Pop. 659.

Galena [guh LEE nuh] (Stone) county seat. First called Jamestown, the name was changed to Galena for the lead mines being developed in that section. *Galena* means "lead ore." The legend that Ponce de Leon in the 16th century discovered ore here, and that it was he who first called it Galena, is untrue (RF). P.O. 1853-now. Pop. 401.

Gallatin [GAL uh tuhn] (Daviess) county seat. This town was named in honor of Albert Gallatin, a financier who served in the cabinets of Thomas Jefferson and James Madison (RF). P.O. 1838-now. Pop. 1,864.

Gallinipper Creek (Johnson). The name of Light Creek was changed because of the large number of gallinippers found there (RF).

Galloway (Greene). This town is one of the few Missouri towns named for a Union Army hero.

Thousands of people turned out when the Galena bridge first opened.

Galt (Grundy). A granddaughter of Zeke Winters, who laid the town out, asserted that it was named for Galt, California, where Winters lived during the Gold Rush. Another source says it was named Gault for an official of the Wabash Railroad. The railroad used the alternative spelling for years (RF). Pop. 296.

Garber (Stone). This post office was named for Joel Garber, who lived in the community (RF). The Rosses, models for characters in <u>The Shepherd of the Hills</u> by Harold Bell Wright, moved here from their more isolated homes to make it easier for the book's admirers to find them. The town depended on the railroad and died as motor travel became more popular (LI).

Gasconade [GAS kuh nayd] or [gas kuh NAYD] (Gasconade). This was once county seat for Gasconade County, and almost became the state capital (RF). P.O. 1823-1825, 1882-1973 (estimated). Pop. 253.

Gasconade County. Nearly one fourth of the state south and west was attached to the original county here, giving it the nickname "State of Gasconade." It is named for the Gasconade River, which empties into the Missouri River within its boundaries (RF). Pop. 14,006.

Gasconade River. This tributary of the Missouri River was first named Blue River. Gasconade comes from a region of France that is famed for its local pride and boastfulness. It therefore reflects the river's swaggering, capricious nature, moving from quiet, deep eddies to rocky rapids. Dru L. Pippin, of the Missouri Conservation Commission, wrote of the river, "Noah Webster gives me special permit by saying that a Gasconader is one who is a 'braggart, given to blustering and boastful talk.' That's me: The Gasconade, a true-blue, one-hundred-percent Missourian."

Gay Feather Prairie (Vernon). The naming committee of the Department of Conservation named this for a prairie plant also known as blazing star.

Gentry County [JEN tree]. The name was given in honor of Richard Gentry who lived in Boone County at the outbreak of the Florida war. On the battlefield of Okeechobee, Colonel Gentry is said to have directed his troops for an hour after he had received a mortal wound (RF). Pop. 6,848.

Germantown (Boone). Started by two German businessmen, this was a prosperous settlement until the Civil War. It was burnt to the ground by southern sympathizers and not rebuilt (APM).

Glasgow [GLAS goh] (Howard). Popularly thought to be named for the Scottish city, the name really came from James Glasgow who, with his son, started a store here and was one of the first settlers (CG). The town was beloved by rivermen who enjoyed the fragrance of its flowers from a mile away (BH). Pop. 1,295.

Goggin's Hog Office (Macon). One of the first settlers of Randolph County fattened his hogs on property southwest of Macon. Sometimes he would come up to check on his hogs, and stay a few days at this primitive outpost at the end of civilization. The name came to mean "as far away as you could get and still be in settled country" (LI).

Golden City (Barton). Tradition says that a few golden nuggets were found by the Spanish when they camped here. They called the place Golden Grove. P.O. 1869-now. Pop. 794.

"Grab-all" (Shelby). This nickname was applied to a part of Shelbyville and dates back to a time when young men would go to "Ribbon Ridge" and snatch the ribbons from young ladies there. Alternatively, the name came from grab-bags that were featured at all the socials (RF).

Humans used Graham Cave for shelter beginning more than 10,000 years ago.

Graham Cave State Park. This was owned by the Graham family when taken over by the state. Radiocarbon dating shows that the shelter cave, which is the principal feature in the park, was inhabited as long as 10,000 years ago (RF).

Granby (Newton). Named for its distinctive rock formation, called the Granby Conglomerate, this boomtown calls itself "The Oldest Mining Town in the Southwest" (LI). In 1853, the Granby stampede lured diggers to lead that was found from 10 to 75 feet below the surface (VR). A local poet was moved to write,

> Millions of money
> They've made, we do think
> Of pure mineral ore,
> Dry-bone and zinc. (LI)

P.O. 1856-1863, 1865-now. Pop. 1,945.

Grand Glaize (Camden). See Auglaize Creek.

Grand Gulf State Park. Often called the "Little Grand Canyon," the gulf was created when the ceiling of a giant cave collapsed. The gulf meanders for a mile through vertical walls as high as 120 feet.

Grand Pass (Saline). This place, town and Missouri Department of Conservation land is named for an old Osage trail that followed the divide for a mile and a half between Salt Fork and the Missouri Bottoms. With the pass never more than five hundred yards wide, there was barely room for the hotel and houses built here (RF). The river changed course, and the narrow strip widened; the name stuck (APM). P.O. 1831-1849, 1888-now. Pop. 53.

Grand River. A tributary of the Missouri River, this was named by the French as early as 1723. It was a popular hunting ground for Native Americans (VR). *Grand*, in this instance, means "beautiful" rather than "large" (LI).

Grandfather Prairie (Pettis). According to Osage tradition, Osage lodges were built to face east to catch the first light of Grandfather the Sun.

Graniteville (Iron). This company-owned town was built for workers in the red-granite quarries here. P.O. 1874-1973.

Grant City
Greasy Cove

Grant City (Worth) county seat. A county board member suggested the name in honor of General Ulysses S. Grant (RF). Republicans in Missouri favored Grant over Lincoln in 1864, the only state to do so (DM). P.O. 1864-now. Pop. 998.

Gravois Creek [GRAV uhz]. The French means "plaster" or "rubbish," but was used to mean "gravelly, rocky" by Mississippi Valley French (RF).

Gravois Mills [GRAV oi MILZ] (Morgan). The Osage people celebrate their heritage at an annual event hosted by the Tribal Council and Chamber of Commerce. The town is named for its mills on the Gravois River. P.O. 1860-now. Pop. 101.

Gravois River. See Gravois Creek.

Gray's Creek. The story goes that this creek was named by a settler who lost a gray mare here one fall and found her next spring, in fine condition (CG).

Grayson (Clinton). Named for the wife of the first land-owner, this little village prospered briefly as a mercantile center but lasted a long time as a community center (APM). The original name was shortened from Graysonville in 1882 by order of the thrifty post office. P.O. 1871-1954.

Greasy Cove [GREE zee]. An American translation for the French *l'anse a la graisse*, this was the cove where New Madrid is located. The name was probably given because of the greasy, sticky, slimy clay mud in the Mississippi River. Occasionally, experts assert that the place, also called Cove of Grease, was so called because of the plentiful bear and beaver there, or because it was where settlers stored greasy bear meat (LI).

Greasy Creek. There are at least six waterways in Missouri named "greasy," probably because of the muddy clay which forms the floor for most of them (RF).

Greene County. By legislative act, this county was named after a Revolutionary War hero like so many other Missouri counties (RF). Organized 1833. Pop. 207,949.

Greenfield (Dade) county seat. When a committee was appointed to find a county seat within four miles of the center of the county it somehow failed to do so. A second was appointed. The commissioners selected this site in 1841 and named the town for its pretty landscapes (RF). P.O. 1850-now. Pop. 1,416.

Greentop (Schuyler). Way before the Women's Lib Movement, this little town elected an entire town government of women in 1935 (VR). P.O. Green Top (earlier spelling) 1849-1857, Greentop 1857-now. Pop. 425.

Greenville (Wayne) county seat. The original town was laid out on a cornfield with streets following rows of corn. It was named for the Ohio town where General Anthony Wayne, the county namesake, concluded a treaty with the Indians in 1795. That town was named by Wayne for General Nathaniel Greene (1742-1786), who started Wayne on his successful military career. When Greenville, Missouri, was flooded by the Wappapello Lake, many buildings including the courthouse were moved (RF). P.O. 1816-1862, 1865-now. Pop. 437.

Grundy County [GRUHN dee]. This name honors a Democratic U.S. senator from Tennessee, the Honorable Felix Grundy. Pop. 10,536.

"Gully Town." This old nickname for Kansas City refers to the many gullies and dry creeks that filled up with water, often preventing floods after a heavy rain. Modern drainage systems have obliterated most of these, and paved others with concrete bottoms (LI).

H

Ha Ha Tonka State Park (Camden). For many years, this was thought to be a made-up name. However, it may have a meaning in a Sioux dialect: *Ha ha* may mean "falls" and *tonka* "big" (JL). The remains of a hewn-stone European-style castle and service buildings are located in the park. P.O. 1895-1937.

Hall's Ferry. First called Music's Ferry, then called Hall's Ferry Landing, this was the site of the first ferry on the Missouri River (CG).

Hallsville (Boone). Named for John W. Hall, the first postmaster, this town is being reborn as a commuter village for Columbia (LI). Pop. 917.

Hamilton (Caldwell). This name has two sources: Alexander Hamilton, American statesman, and Joseph Hamilton, a lawyer and soldier killed in the Revolutionary War. The young James Cash Penney worked here for a mercantile store. His chain of J.C. Penney stores was built on a foundation of work ethic and reinvestment (LI). P.O. 1858-now. Pop. 1,737.

Handy (Ripley). The post office application may have said "Haney," for Noah Haney's country store here. But folks also thought the name appropriate, because it was handy to get the mail here rather than going the long distance to Pine (APM). P.O. 1913-1954.

Hannibal [HAN uh buhl] (Marion). Hannibal was an African general who fought in a Roman war on Carthage. How his name got to Missouri is a mystery. In about 1800, Don Antonio Soulard, a Spaniard, called the creeks here Hannibal, Scipio and Fabius. Soulard may have used existing names or made up his own. The names are all from Roman history (RF). Charles Dickens poked fun at classical names when he gave the name New Thermopylae to Hannibal in his book <u>Martin Chuzzlewit</u>. Mark Twain also had fun with Hannibal, calling it St. Petersburg after the Russian capital. Later, Hannibal Creek was renamed Bear Creek, but the town remained Hannibal. See also Antioch, "New Thermopylae." P.O. 1820-now. Pop. 18,004.

Hannibal and St. Joseph Railroad. The first railroad across the state, it linked the eastern United States with the western frontier at the important port of Hannibal.

Happy Hollow. This name is used several places in the state, given as an ideal name or as a pioneer name poking fun at residents. In at least two places (Crawford, Warren), the place was the site of whiskey stills (RF).

Harmony Mission. See Batesville.

Harrison County [HAR uh sn]. This was named after Albert G. Harrison (1800-1839), who was one of the first two members of Congress elected from Missouri. Harrison died while serving his term (RF). Organized 1845. Pop. 8,469.

Harrisonville (Cass) county seat. Named for Albert G. Harrison (see Harrison County), this was a hub of border warfare where the Younger family had a large farm (VR). P.O. 1854-now. Pop. 7,683.

Hartsburg (Boone). This was named, as was Hart Creek, for a settler (CG). With the demise of river and train travel, the rhythm of the town has slowed dramatically. Before the advent of the car, the town had two banks, a newspaper and all of the other amenities of a self-sustaining town. Today it is known for its Pumpkin Festival held each October that draws more than 5,000 people. Pop. 131.

Hartville (Wright) county seat. This was named for Isaac Hart, early hunter and settler (RF). P.O. 1842-1863, 1865-now. Pop. 539.

Hawk Point (Lincoln). One of the few Bohemian communities in the mid-1840s, it took over the community of Mashek (Enc). It was named because it was a place where hawks were common (RF). P.O. 1840-now. Pop. 472.

Hayti [HAY teye] (Pemiscot). This town was a refuge for escaped African American slaves; after the Civil War it became home to free people. It is named for the island in the West Indies (RF). P.O. 1895-now. Pop. 3,280.

Headquarters (Stoddard). This imposing name was given by the president of the Moss Tie Company, maker of railroad ties, for the headquarters of his company (RF). P.O. 1895-1900.

Heather (Marion). This post office and general store was named for a landowner, H. Clay Heather, who served as both representative and senator in Jefferson City (RF). P.O. 1901-1906.

Helena [huh LEE nuh] (Andrew). This is one of several Missouri towns named for the daughter of a railroad official. P.O. 1880-now. Pop. 162.

Hell-on-the-Line (Barton). The peacefully named Berry Hill became a drink-and-fight town when nearby Kansas passed prohibition and Missouri still allowed liquor (APM).

Hematite [HEM uh teyet] (Jefferson). A small iron mine operated near here, so the town took the name for iron ore (RF). P.O. 1858-now.

Hempland (Lafayette). In this section of the county, hemp was grown to be made into rope. P.O. 1857-1860.

Henry County [HEN ree]. First called Rives County, this was renamed to honor Patrick Henry, the Revolutionary War hero that said, "Give me liberty or give me death." Organized 1834. Pop. 20,044.

Herculaneum [huhr kyuh LAY ni uhm] (Jefferson). Platted by Moses Austin and Samuel Hammond, this lead-mining town was named for a Roman town which was being excavated at the time. Local tradition says the name was particularly apt because the smoke from the smelters looked like Mt. Vesuvius erupting (GS). P.O. 1811-1858, 1890-now. Pop. 2,263.

Hermann (Gasconade). Hermann was founded in 1836 by the German Settlement Society of Philadelphia, whose members were appalled at the loss of customs and language among their countrymen in America (LI). This "Second Fatherland" was intended to be a self-supporting refuge. It was set up as a joint-stock company and advertised throughout the United States and Germany. On behalf of the society, one member acquired 11,300 acres for $15,612. His choice for the site, bounded by hills and bluffs on three sides and the Missouri River on the north and teeming with wild grapevines, was influenced by its similarity to the Rhine River region in Germany. The Society modeled the layout of the colony on that of Philadelphia. A variety of professionals, artisans and laborers were drawn by the idea. Selecting the name of Germany's national hero Hermann (*Arminius* in Latin), who defeated the Roman legion in 9 A.D., seemed fitting for the great dream their new settlement embodied (BD). P.O. 1838-now. Pop. 2,754.

German place names

Because place names mark our world from the day we first learn to speak, they seem solid and enduring. But if the study of place names teaches nothing else it reminds us that history changes all things—even the way we identify ourselves and our places. The German experience in Missouri gives us a good example.

In 1829, a book describing the wonders and beauty of Missouri was published in Germany. Report on a Journey to the Western States of North America was a best-seller. "I do not conceal the fact from you that the entire life of the inhabitants of these regions seemed to me like a dream at first," wrote Gottfried Duden. "Even now, after I have had three months to examine conditions more closely, it seems to me almost a fantasy when I consider what nature offers man here." Duden described acorns as big as hen's eggs, and grapevines laden with sweet fruit.

To the struggling, even starving, German-speaking European at home, the allure of freedom and plenty in America was irresistible. Thousands of German-speaking settlers emigrated to Missouri. Settling mostly along the Mississippi River south of St. Louis and the Missouri River from St. Louis to Boonville, especially south of the river, they created what one geographer calls the "German Arc." That area along the Missouri River is often referred to, even today, as "The Missouri Rhineland." Besides bringing their place names, the settlers brought religion, music, foods, industry and tradition with them. Many years before the Christmas tree was adopted by Anglo settlers, there are records of that tradition in German-Missouri homes.

German-speaking settlers often named their settlements for the places they had left. In Perry County, Missouri's first German Lutheran immigrants (1839) arrived, partly inspired by Duden's book. They created Altenburg, Dresden, Frohna, Seelitz and Wittenberg, named for towns in Germany. Other German place names are sprinkled around the state: Detmold, Dissen, Hermann, Kiel and New Offenburg, for example.

JULY 20, 2008

German place names
continued

Some German-speaking settlers pledged that they would retain their language and customs, but most families came to the territory determined to become productive Americans. They often named their towns with idealistic or patriotic names like Freedom, Hope, Liberty, Useful and Welcome.

By the Civil War, dozens of rural German communities were in place, complete with schools, churches, fraternal organizations, stores and post offices. Generally abolitionists, the German-speaking Missourians found themselves at odds with the southern settlers who had come before. Missouri was particularly divided during the Civil War.

During World War I, with anti-German feeling strong, many German Americans felt they should assert their American identities. The German language was abandoned in schools and churches and some residents of German places felt that they should change their names. Madison County's German Township became Marquand and Gasconade County's town of Potsdam became Pershing. There were motions to change the name of Bismarck to Loyal and Kaiser to Success. Citizens of Diehlstadt considered changing its name to Liberty. These three changes were resisted.

By World War II, the descendants of these German Americans felt rightly secure in their homeland. The German names on our landscape have endured as markers in our history.

Information gleaned from the writings of
Adolf Schroeder and Walter Schroeder.

Hermitage (Hickory) county seat. The commissioners chose the county seat name before they decided on a site; the town is named for the Tennessee residence of Andrew Jackson. Later there was a rivalry between the east and west sides of the county and several elections over a change of location, but the issue was decided each time in favor of Hermitage. See also Jackson County, Hickory County. P.O. 1848-now. Pop. 512.

Hi Lonesome Prairie (Barton). The Department of Conservation naming committee was inspired by the prairies of the west that were so vast they made a man feel small. See Friendly Prairie.

Hi Wassie (Oregon). The Cherokee came into Missouri in 1818 and 1819, and brought this place name from their homeland in the East (RF). Nearby Low Wassie Creek was probably a pioneer joking name that played off this one (RF).

Hibernia. See Cedar City.

Hickory County [HIK uh ree]. Named for President Andrew "Old Hickory" Jackson, this county was organized the year of his death (RF). Jackson was said to be strong and tough like hickory wood. See Hermitage, Jackson County. Organized 1845. Pop. 7,335.

High Hill (Montgomery). The post office moved from its high location (present-day Jonesburg) to the present one. The old location was one of the highest points between Kansas City and Saint Louis (RF). Some folks have forgotten the old location and insist that the town is at the summit of a long, slow grade and was given by railroad workers (LI). P.O. (Warren) 1837, (Montgomery) 1837-now. Pop. 204.

High Ridge (Jefferson). According to radio operators, this is an appropriate name for one of Missouri's high points (LI). It is the highest point in Jefferson County (RF).

Hillsboro (Jefferson) county seat. More centrally located than Herculaneum, the first seat of county government, this town's original name was Monticello, for the home of Thomas Jefferson. Finding there was another Monticello in Missouri, the name was changed to Hillsborough for the hill just south of town. The spelling was changed to Hillsboro to simplify. P.O. 1892-now. Pop. 1,625.

Hocomo
Honey Creek

Hocomo [HOH kuh moh] (Howell). This name was created from the first two letters of each word: Howell County, MO. P.O. 1931-now.

Hog Shoal (Pulaski). About 20 miles north of Hazelton on the Big Piney River, this dangerous place "hogged" log rafts being floated by raftsmen from lumber camps to market (GA).

Holland (Pemiscot). Like the country, this town was built on submerged land that has been reclaimed (Enc). P.O. 1900-now. Pop. 237.

Hollister (Taney). Named for a railroad man who was a friend of the developer, this resort town was planned to look like a charming English village. Visitors arriving by train saw the hotel and shops, built in the British half-timbered style from stone, stucco and wood. Platted in 1906 by William J. Johnson, a landscape architect, the plan takes advantage of the natural beauty of the limestone hills with terraces, parks and supporting walls of stone (VR). P.O. 1904-now. Pop. 2,628.

Hollywood (Dunklin). First called Klondike, a hopeful name given by railroad promoters to evoke images of the gold rush region in Alaska, the name changed because of the holly trees growing there. P.O. 1898-1974.

Holt County [HOHLT]. Part of the Platte Purchase, this county was named after State Representative Dr. David Rice Holt who died while in office. In those days before the professional politician, Holt was a minister and a physician, successful in both fields (RF). Organized 1841. Pop. 6,034.

Homeless Junction (Scott). In the 1930s, tenant farmers in southwest Missouri were under pressure from all sides. Mechanized farming required fewer people on the land, farm prices were low, and there was a drought. Landowners were forcing tenants (mostly the descendents of slaves) off the land. After dramatic protests, some were relocated; others were gathered by government officials to this settlement (LI).

Honey Creek (Cole). While the Cole County creek may bear a family name, there have been three towns and at least seven waterways named Honey Creek in Missouri. The name recalls days when hunting for honey trees was profitable. See Bee Creek. P.O. (Newton) 1843-unknown, (McDonald) unknown-1863, 1867-1871, Honey Creek (Cole) 1888-1893. Pop. 30.

Hoop Pole College (or Hoop Pole School) (Scotland). People here made their living by cutting and shaving hoops for barrels (APM).

Hoozaw River (Warren). Hoozaw is one variation of the Native American name now standardized as Osage. See Osage.

Houston [HYOO stuhn] (Texas) county seat. Located in the geographical center of the county, the town was named after Sam Houston, politician and the hero of the battle of San Jacinto in which he avenged the Alamo massacre (RF). At time of settlement, the county was in a kind of Texas frenzy, because many of the settler's sons had gone with Moses Austin to settle there. Houston was completely destroyed during the Civil War and rebuilt when the war ended. P.O. 1846-1863, 1865-now. Pop. 2,118.

Houstonia (Pettis). This town was laid out by Thomas F. Houston, who settled here in 1851. P.O. 1872-now. Pop. 283.

Howard County [HOW uhrd]. This was nicknamed "The Mother of Counties" because its land was divided into all or part of thirty-six counties of Missouri and Iowa. Of Missouri's first fifteen governors, eight came from Howard County (VR). It is named for General Benjamin Howard, governor of Upper Louisiana, which became Missouri Territory on June 4, 1812. Organized 1816. Pop. 9,631.

Howell County [HOW uhl]. This was named by early settlers in Howell Valley, which in turn was named after Thomas Jefferson Howell. He represented Oregon County in the legislature and was important in getting Howell County organized (RF). Organized 1857. Pop. 31,447.

Humansville (Polk). The name was given for James G. Human, city founder (LI). Pop. 1,084.

Hume (Bates). First called Howard, the name was changed when three barrels of whiskey from the Hume distillery arrived here instead of their destination in Howard, Kansas. Appreciative citizens changed the town name to that of the distillery. P.O. 1880-now. Pop. 287.

Hungry Mother Creek. A local resident says he can remember an old woman begging for food here (LI). Another story: Settlers named this place "Hunger's Mother" after a hard winter (RF).

Hunkah Prairie
Huzzah State Forest

Hunkah Prairie (Barton). This Missouri Department of Conservation prairie was named for a branch of the Osage tribe (LI).

Huntsdale (Boone). For an early settler, William Bunch Hunt (CG), this town was almost lost in the floods of 1993. P.O. 1892-1953.

Huntsville (Randolph) county seat. Named for Daniel Hunt, a Kentuckian and one of the first settlers, the town had a brief prosperity due to coal mining, but the mines quickly declined. Jack Conroy described Huntsville in his novel The Disinherited (VR). P.O. 1831-now. Pop. 1,567.

Hurricane Creek. There are eight creeks so-named in Missouri, most associated with violent tornadoes, once called hurricanes here. Missouri averages 27 tornadoes per year, but in record-breaking 1973 we had 79. Other Hurricane names, like Camden County's Hurricane Deck, are likewise explained. One Hurricane Creek (Bollinger) is named for its violent nature after a heavy rain; it is dangerous or impossible to cross. A town, Hurricane, was located nearby (RF). P.O. 1894-1942.

Huzzah Creek [HOO zah] or [HOO zaw] (Crawford). This name is a variation of the Native American name now called Osage. See Osage.

Huzzah State Forest (St. Charles). See Huzzah Creek.

I

Iantha [EYE an thuh] (Barton). This is a name of classical origin. Iantha was the daughter of Oceanus and Tethys; Lord Byron's popular <u>Childe Harold's Pilgrimmage</u> is dedicated to her (APM). P.O. 1881-now.

Ilasco [uh LAS koh] (Ralls). Named by a local cement company, the letters stand for iron, lead, aluminum, silicon, calcium and oxygen, the main ingredients in concrete (GS). P.O. 1919-1960.

Illmo [IL moh] (Scott). This town is on the border of Illinois and Missouri (Enc). It owes its existence to the railroad, which built a bridge across the Mississippi River here. The name combines Ill for Illinois and Mo for Missouri (APM). P.O. 1904-now.

Imperial (Jefferson). This town was referred to as West Kimmswick, but took the name Imperial to imply that it was of superior quality (RF). During World War I, the name was changed to Liberty to be rid of the association with the Imperial Powers (RF). After the war, the old name was reinstated. This is the home of Mastodon State Park, one of North America's largest sites for Ice Age people and mastodons. P.O. 1951-now. Pop. 4,156.

Impo (Texas). Two stories here: (1) The post office rejected the name Dunn, which was the name of the settlement. The postmaster submitted the name Important, which was shortened by the ever-thrifty postal department to its present form. (2) The townspeople met to discuss the rejected name Dunn. In searching for a name, one of them noticed there were two kinds of oatmeal stocked by the storekeeper—Imperial and Mother's. The first letters of these two names, followed by P.O. for post office, gave the town its name (RF). P.O. 1919-1955.

Independence
Iron County

Independence [in duh PEN duhns] (Jackson) county seat. Today, the "Queen City of the Trails" (LI) is Missouri's fourth largest town. As an outfitting center for trappers and hunters and an important center of trade with Mexico, its official name was given in commemoration of the Declaration of Independence (RF). P.O. 1827-now. Pop. 112,301.

Ink (Shannon). When a community meeting was called to name this post office/general store, citizens stayed late arguing and agonizing. They had been told to keep the name short, and ran through a child's ABC reader without success. Finally, the problem was solved when somebody spilled a bottle of you-know-what. The meeting was adjourned. A second story tells simply that the postmaster wrote down all the three-letter names he could think of. A third story tells he was disturbed because a shipment had been ruined by a spilled bottle of ink. Which story is true? We'll never know. P.O. 1885-1954.

Irish Settlement (Oregon and Ripley). Also known as Irish Wilderness, this place was purchased by a priest in the 1850s to be home for poor Irish, many of whom had escaped persecution in Ireland. The land cost 12.5 cents per acre. A settlement was established but devastated in the Civil War. A post office here, named Wilderness, had a long existence.

Iron County [EYE uhrn]. (1) This county was named for the iron found there (RF). (2) Iron was supposed to run underneath the county in its entirety, and many early smelters were located here (DM). Organized 1857. Pop. 10,726.

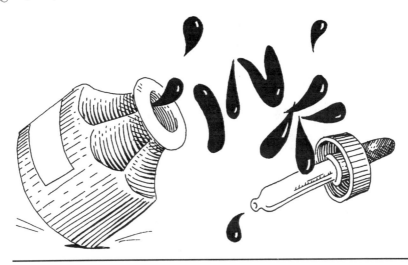

Iron Mountain (St. Francois). The mountain was once thought to be solid iron. A town nearby has also taken the name (APM). P.O. 1846-1894, 1906-1978.

Ironton (Iron) county seat. The town was named for the county and the county's principal export. U.S. General Grant arrived in this industrial part of the state in 1861 and quickly raised a division of 3,000 troops (RF). P.O. 1858-now. Pop. 1,539.

Island City (Gentry). First called Couchtown, after a local family, this improbably named village was surrounded by land (LI). In Mississippi French, the word *ile*, meaning "island," acquired the meaning "grove," so some land-bound places bear the word (GS). This may have been translated to form the name of this town. P.O. 1858-1906.

J

Jack (Dent). The first post office here was first called Nursery Hill because of a large plant nursery, then re-established and named for the son of the first postmaster. P.O. 1905-1954.

Jackass Bend. This bend in the Missouri River was particularly hard on mules. One story tells that a preacher and his mule were passengers on a boat that hit a sandbar here. The mule jumped into the water, pulling in a shipmate, who was drowned. Another story tells that a load of mules bound for Fort Leavenworth overturned here. Another speculation is that the tricky bend made a jackass of many a boat pilot (CG).

Jacks Fork River. The post office here is named for the river. P.O. 1917-1954.

Jackson [JAK sn] (Cape Girardeau) county seat. First called Birdstown for a prominent family, three new names were suggested for the county seat. Each of the suggestions was for a local family. To avoid conflict, the name was changed to honor Andrew Jackson, who was one of the state's heroes. See also Jackson County. P.O. 1811-now. Pop. 9,256.

Jackson County. First called "The Blue Country," most of the land in the western part of this county was acquired directly from Native Americans by treaty in 1825 (RF). This county was the nation's first to claim the name of the President Andrew Jackson, victorious military commander at the Battle of New Orleans and seventh president of the United States. Nineteen Missouri townships were named for him (RF), and many Missourians called themselves "Jackson Democrats." Organized 1826. Pop. 633,232.

Jackson Twister (Texas). This unexpected turn in the Big Piney River hung up a raft manned by "the Jackson boys." They lost a day freeing it, and gave the name to this place 11 miles north of Hazelton (GA).

Jacksonville (Randolph). This town was named for Hancock Jackson, pre-Civil War governor of Missouri (VR). Hancock Jackson was elected lieutenant governor in 1857 (RF). P.O. 1837-1840, 1859-now. Pop. 115.

Jamesport (Daviess). The name comes from its two founders, James Gillilan and James Allen. There is no port, but the two James are reputed to have been "sports" (LI). P.O. 1857-now. Pop. 570.

Japan (Franklin). After the bombing of Pearl Harbor, citizens wanted to change this name. They relented when they learned its story. It was named for a church which was named for Japanese Christians killed for their faith. The town and the church kept their names, but local people once pronounced the name JAY-pan to separate themselves from the country. P.O. 1860-1868, 1887-1908. Pop. 50.

Jasper County [JAS puhr]. Sergeant William Jasper, a Revolutionary War hero, replaced a fallen flag on Fort Moultrie but lost his life trying to replace the colors on Spring Hill, near Savannah, Georgia, on October 7, 1779. Organized 1841. Pop. 90,465.

Jefferson County [JEF uhr sn]. This name was chosen for President Thomas Jefferson because he was responsible for the Louisiana Purchase, which brought our territory under American ownership (RF). Organized 1818. Pop. 171,380.

Jefferson City (Cole) county seat. Named by government officials who first chose the name Missouriopolis, the City of Jefferson became the first town in the United States to be named for Thomas Jefferson (LI). Missouri's first state capitol was located in St. Charles nearer the confluence of the Missouri River and the Mississippi during the era of river trade. See St. Charles. The current capitol building was built in 1913 after the previous capitol building was destroyed by a lightning fire in 1911 (BD). The Capitol building was constructed *under* budget. Leftover funds were used to commission artists to decorate the structure. The interior of the Capitol is a pictoral walk through Missouri's past, brought to life through the work of Frank Brangwyn, N.C. Wyeth, James Earle Fraser, Alexander Stirling Calder and the Thomas Hart Benton (BD). P.O. 1823-now. Pop. 35,517.

Jennings (St. Louis). This railroad town, now a commuter town for St. Louis, is named for a family. P.O. 1874-1901. Pop. 15,841.

Jerico Springs
Joplin

Jerico Springs (Cedar). The enterprising J.B. Carrico platted this town on his land, and named it for himself and the Bible's Jericho. P.O. 1905-now. Pop. 247.

Joachim Creek (Jefferson). The creek may be named for a neighbor family. It also may be a reference to Joachim, traditionally identified as father of the Virgin Mary. He is not mentioned in the Bible (LI).There are two pronunciations: Used by the French, the name sounds sort of like "SWAH shin," and it is often spelled Swashing or Swashin. Another pronunciation, attributed to the Germans, is "YOH kum."

Johannisberg (Perry). This settlement has disappeared except in local memory. It was an offshoot of Perry County's Dresden. See Altenburg and Dresden. The name is probably derived from the parish name of the original leader of the migration (RF).

Johnson County [JAHN sn]. Richard Mentor Johnson (1780-1850) was born near Louisville, Kentucky, served in the War of 1812, and at the Battle of Thames in 1813. A popular politician, he served as vice president for one term; his ticket was defeated in 1840 (RF). Organized 1834. Pop. 42,514.

Johnson's Shut-Ins State Park. Over centuries, the Black River has carved canyon-like gaps or shut-ins in some of the oldest exposed rock in Missouri. A "shut-in" is a waterway with steep banks.

Jonesburg (Montgomery). This town was named for James Jones, a North Carolinian who built a log house here in 1828 and six years later established the Cross Keys Tavern, a stopping place on the Boon's Lick Trail (VR). P.O. 1893-now. Pop. 630.

Joplin [JAH plin] (Newton and Jasper). This was named for the first Methodist minister in the area. In 1870, lead was discovered near Joplin and three years later, there was a city of 4,000 where there had been prairie. Thirty years later, it had 26,000 people. P.O. 1871-1872, 1877-now. Pop. 40,866.

K

Kahoka [kuh HOH kuh] (Clark) county seat. High on a rolling prairie in a prosperous agricultural district, this town was frequently called Round Prairie (VR). Kahoka was named for a tribe of Native Americans sometimes called *Gawakie*, or "the lean ones." The tribe roamed over this part of Missouri and northern Illinois (RF). P.O. 1861-now. Pop. 2,195.

Kaiser (Miller) This is a family name. During World War I, there was a movement by citizens to change the name of this town to Success, to avoid association with the German enemy. P.O. 1904-now. Pop. 200.

Kansas City [KAN suhs] or [KAN zuhs] (Jackson, Clay, Platte, Cass). Missouri's largest city, this was known as "the city built on beef and bread" for its stockyards and wheat-shipping industry and nicknamed "Gully Town" for its many ravines (see "Gully Town"). There was an early French trading town, Kawsmouth, here, but it was flooded in 1844 and the site aban-

doned. Later, the first official name was Town of Kansas, then City of Kansas, then the present form. The name comes from the Kansas (or Kaw) River. See Kansas River. P.O. 1861-now. Pop. 435,146.

Kansas River. The river is named for a Native American nation that lived nearby. The name was spelled Kanza or Kanzas, or *Riviere des Cans* by the French. The French pronunciation sounded like "Kaw" to the Americans, who often spelled it that way (RF). It empties into the Missouri River.

Kate Howard Chute. On the Missouri River one mile below the Osage, the steamer *Kate Howard* sank here. A second, the *Excel*, followed later.

Katy Trail, The. Some of the rail bed for the old Missouri, Kansas and Texas Railroad has been converted to a trail for walking and biking. This rails-to-trails conversion is one of the nation's longest, stretching for close to 200 miles through the Missouri River Valley. Also known as the MK&T Trail, where the original Katy Railroad ran beginning in the 1890s.

Kaw Bend. This bend on the Gasconade was home to one Native American who moved from the reservation to this place to find peace (BH).

Kearney [KAHR nee] or [KAIR nee] (Clay). Birthplace of Jesse James, and site of his grave, this town was originally called Centerville. The population was dispersed during the Civil War, and rebuilt when the Hannibal and St. Joe Railroad came through. The new town was named for Fort Kearney, Nebraska (APM). P.O. 1868-now. Pop. 2,260.

Keith's Rock. This rock in the Gasconade was the site of the wreck of the *Lancaster*, a steamboat piloted by Captain George Keith.

Kennett [KEN uht] (Dunklin) county seat. The citizens protested that Chilliticoux, the original town name, was too long and tough to spell; it had been selected because it was the name of a Delaware chief who lived nearby. The name was changed in 1848 to Butler, for F.C. Butler, who helped select this as a site for the seat of government. The name was again changed when postal authorities thought Butler could be confused with Butler County. The new name was Kennett, for Luther Kennett, mayor of St. Louis, who promoted the idea of railroads in Missouri (RF). P.O. 1860-1863, 1867-now. Pop. 10,941.

Keytesville [KEETS vil] (Chariton) county seat. Mr. James Keyte, English founder of the town, built a log cabin in 1831 as a post office, but no town was incorporated until 1868. The county seat was at that time located at Old Chariton, a promising village. The first official courthouse building, however, in the county was in Keytesville (RF). P.O. 1831-now. Pop. 564.

Kimberly (Randolph). Although the name may honor a person, it is also believed to be for an African city that was well known to Americans because of the Boer War (GS). P.O. 1900-1905.

Kimmswick (Jefferson). Founded by Theodore Kimm, this river town had importance as a shipping point for Pilot Knob and Iron Mountain until the smelter was closed. The town's decline was a lucky break for its future. Today, its log cabins house restaurants and shops, and its location south of St. Louis makes it popular with tourists. The town has adopted the motto "The Best Kept Secret." P.O. 1858-1973. Pop. 135.

King Bee (Ripley). The residents of this town thought it would be an important city. They named it, mistakenly, after the bee they thought ruled the hive (LI). Also spelled Kingbee.

King City (Gentry). Citizens wished to call this Petersburg, but there was another so named in the state. The postmaster, Mr. King, then named it after himself. Pop. 986.

Kingdom City (Callaway). See Kingdom of Callaway. P.O. 1970-now. Pop. 112.

"Kingdom of Callaway" [KAL uh way]. This is a nickname given to the county which withdrew from both the Union and the Confederacy. The story goes that all the young men in the county had left to fight with the South when the word came in October 1861, that Union troops

were very close. This news terrified the people left at home—mostly women, children and old men. Troops on the march could destroy a family's supplies for the winter. All the county's boys and old men gathered together, armed with hunting rifles and logs painted to look like cannons. Seeing the display, the Union commander quickly promised not to bother the county. The home guard in return promised not to side with the Confederacy. Word was sent to Jefferson City and Washington, D.C., that the county had become a kingdom and would not join either side (LI).

Kingshighway. By 1789, enough towns had been built next to the river so that there was need for a road. To the fur traders, the road was a symbol that they were taking over the land as well as the water. They wanted it to have an important-sounding name. It was called in Spanish *El Camino Real*, or "royal road," and it followed a Native American trail from St. Louis to New Madrid. The French called it *Rue Royale*, but it was the American name that we know today. Parts of the road are still in use, following U.S. Route 55 along the Mississippi River.

Kingston (Caldwell) county seat. This town was named in honor of Austin A. King, who was afterwards governor of the state (RF). King worked to bring railroads to Missouri, and was rewarded near the end of his term with the opening of the first passenger train here. P.O. 1843-now. Pop. 279.

Kirksville (Adair) county seat. Jesse Kirk, an early settler, promised the surveyors a turkey dinner and whiskey if the town could be named for him (RF). P.O. 1843-now. Pop. 17,152.

Kirkwood (St. Louis). In 1853, a group of St. Louis businessmen platted this town on the Missouri Pacific line and named it for James P. Kirkwood, chief engineer of the Missouri Pacific Railroad (VR). P.O. 1854-1901. Pop. 27,291.

Knob Noster [NAHB NAHS tuhr] (Johnson). Two prominent mounds (also called "knobs") in the prairie give this town its Latin-like name; *noster* means "our," so the translation is supposed to be "our knobs" (Enc). P.O. 1846-now. Pop. 2,261.

Knox County [NAHKS]. This county was settled quickly, because of its well-watered, undulating prairie. It was named for Henry Knox, a Boston bookseller, who became George Washington's chief of artillery during the

Revolutionary War, and served as the first secretary of war for the United States (1785-1794) (RF). Organized 1845. Pop. 4,482.

Krakow [KRAY kow] or [KRAY koh] (Franklin). The first Polish newspaper in the United States, the <u>Polish Eagle</u> was printed here, and the publisher named the community after the Polish city (LI). P.O. 1871-1876, 1883-1953.

L

La Charrette (Warren). The first white village in the region was settled near the banks of Charrette Creek in 1766 by French fur trappers. It was named for the creek.

La Petite Gemme Prairie. A name pulled out of the air by the naming committee of the Department of Conservation, this means "the little gem" in French.

La Plata [lah PLAY tuh] (Macon). Researchers have said that the name means "wrought iron" (APM) or "wrought silver" (DE), and, indeed, there were many foundries in Macon County. Two men drew straws for the privilege of naming this town; the losing man would have called it Charlotsville for his favorite sister (RF). According to The 1888 Handbook of Macon County, this town is in the "midst of a royal farm region" and home to "1,100 wide-awake and progressive people" (LI). P.O. 1856-now. Pop. 1,401.

Labadie [LAB uh dee] (Franklin). While hunting with his 12-year-old son, Sylvester L'Abbadie shot a bear and chased it into a cave near here. After waiting for his father to return, the son went for help, but search parties were unable to find the cave. Years later, an explorer found the cave and, within, the skeletons of man and bear. The cave from then on was known as Labadie Cave. The town name came from the cave (CG). P.O. 1855-now.

Laclede County [luh KLEED]. This county, and many Missouri schools, were named for Pierre LaClede, early explorer and founder of St. Louis (RF). Organized 1849. Pop. 27,158.

Laddonia [luh DOHN yuh] (Audrain). First named Mutton Town for its herds of sheep, this was later officially named for Amos Ladd, one of the founders (VR). P.O. 1871-now. Pop. 581.

Ladue (St. Louis). This town was named for a local judge. Pop. 8,847.

Lafayette County [laf ee YET] or [LAY fee yet]. First named Cooper County in honor of Searshell Cooper, Indian fighter, the name was changed to Lillard for James Lillard, one of the first members of the state legislature. An abusive letter written by Lillard, who had become disgusted with Missouri, caused the county to reconsider, and it changed its name to honor the French general who spent a year in the United States and visited all 24 states including Missouri, then only four years old (RF). Organized 1820. Pop. 31,107.

Lake of the Ozarks. Named for its location, this lake was formed by impounding the Osage River and flooding the deeply eroded valleys (VR). The jagged shoreline of 1,300 miles gives it more lakefront footage than Lake Michigan.

Lake Ozark (Miller). When the dam created Lake of the Ozarks, some towns were destroyed by the water but others were created. This post office, called Lakeside, soon changed its name to reflect its location. Today it is a thriving tourist town. P.O. 1932-now. Pop. 681.

Lake Sherwood (Warren). In this wooded subdivision homes are grouped around several man-made lakes. It was named by promoters to evoke images of densely wooded Sherwood Forest. Pop. 300.

Lake St. Louis (St. Charles). This is a planned residential area with its own lake. It is an easy commute to the city 30 miles away. Pop. 7,400.

Lake Taneycomo. The oldest reservoir west of the Mississippi River, this 24-mile-long lake was created by a dam impounding waters of the White River (VR). The name is a combination of its abbreviated location names: Taney County (CO), Missouri (MO).

Lake Wappapello (or Wappapello Lake) (Wayne). This 6,000-acre lake is the second largest in Missouri, created for flood control. Many towns were moved when the dam was built. See Wappapello.

Lakota [LAY koh tuh] (Cooper). In Teton Sioux dialect, this means "friendly allies" (JL). P.O. 1902-1906.

Lamar (Barton). Founded in 1856 and named for Mirabeau B. Lamar, president of the Texas Republic. This is the birthplace of the man who said "Being a President is like riding a tiger. A man has to keep on riding or be swallowed," Harry Truman. P.O. 1853-1863, 1866-now. Pop. 4,168.

Lambert Field. The St. Louis airport is named for Major Albert Bond Lambert, a pioneer balloonist who established the first Army balloon school in 1917 in St. Louis (LI).

Lamine River [luh MEYEN] or [luh MEEN]. The origin is thought to be a 1714 writing of French explorer Sieur de Bourgmond who noted that the "Indians take lead from a mine." A 1720 map calls it "Riviere de la Mine" or "River of the Mine" (VR).

Lancaster [LANG kuh stuhr] (Schuyler) county seat. This town was probably named by an Ohioan in honor of his native town in Lancaster, Ohio (RF). In the late 1800s and early 1900s, this was home of "Diamond Billy" Hall, a circus promoter who shipped zebras, elephants and other exotic animals all over the world. P.O. 1846-now. Pop. 785.

Last Chance (Barton). This was the last station on the Frisco Railroad in Missouri before crossing the line into Kansas.

Lawrence County [LAH ruhns]. Named for Captain James Lawrence who lost his life in the Revolutionary War (RF). Although wounded and dying, he encouraged his comrades with the quotable, "Don't give up the ship." Organized 1845. Pop. 30,236.

Leadwood (St. Francois). Originally called Owl Creek for a nearby creek, the name was coined to reflect the business of lead mining in a wooded setting. P.O. 1903-1966. Pop. 1,247.

Leadwood Access (St. Francois). Originally named Claude DuTisne Access, after an early French explorer, the Department of Conservation changed the name when people complained they couldn't pronounce DuTisne. (It's [doo TEEN].) Leadwood is the name of a nearby town.

Lebanon [LEB uh nuhn] (Laclede) county seat. This was named after Lebanon, Tennessee, from which many of the settlers had come. Because townspeople refused to donate money and land to build a depot, the railroad station was built about three miles from the town, which gradually moved to meet it. The sections are still referred to as old and new towns (RF). Earlier, the name was claimed by towns in Boone (1837-1842) and Camden (1850-unknown). P.O. unknown-now. Pop. 9,983.

Lecoma (Dent). Named for its founders: Lenox, Comstock and Martin (GS). P.O. 1883-now.

Lee's Summit [LEEZ SUH mit] or [LEE SUH mit] (Jackson, Cass). During the border wars of the Civil War era, Dr. Pleasant Lea was kidnapped by bushwhackers here. The incident is remembered in the place name which, unfortunately, misspells Lea's name. Cole Younger is buried here, having died of old age, and not from one of the 24 gunshot wounds he received in his life (LI). The town is on one of the highest points between St. Louis and Kansas City (hence the name Summit). It is the state's ninth most populous city. P.O. 1865-1866, 1868-now. Pop. 46,418.

Lewis County [LOO is]. Meriwether Lewis (1774-1809), native of Virginia, in 1804 was selected as a leader for an expedition to explore the country west of the Mississippi River. In the two years that the expedition was absent, they traveled all the way to the Pacific Ocean and returned safely. Their safe return proved that settlement in the West was possible.

Civil War buffs rendezvous each year in Lexington
to relive the Battle of Lexington.

Lewiston
Lickskillet

In 1807, Captain Lewis was made governor of Missouri Territory and died while in office (RF). See Clark County. Organized 1833. Pop. 10,233.

Lewiston (Montgomery). This town was named for Meriwether Lewis (LI). See Lewis County. P.O. 1825-1837. Pop. 453.

Lexington (Lafayette) county seat. Named for Lexington, Kentucky (VR), reminders of the Civil War are still visible here. There is a cannonball in a courthouse pillar, and the trenches and earthworks of the Battle of Lexington have never been covered or cultivated (LI). P.O. 1831-now. Pop. 4,860.

Liberal (Barton). This successful community was founded by G.H. Walser for people who wished to live without any religious doctrine or sects. Citizens accepted "the world our home, our brethren all mankind," and allowed no churches within the settlement (APM). P.O. 1880-now. Pop. 604.

Liberty (Clay) county seat. Two ideas: (1) This town was platted in 1822, not long after the American Revolution, hence the name (RF). (2) The first lots were sold on the 4th of July, 1822 (APM). P.O. 1829-now. Pop. 20,459.

Liberty Bend (Jackson). This treacherous bend in the Missouri River was eliminated by the Corps of Engineers, who dug a canal one mile long to cut off five miles of river. The engineers constructed a bridge on dry land, then dug the canal under it (CG).

Lick Branch, Fork or **Creek**. Named for the spots where deer or buffalo came to lick the minerals that were carried by water and dried on the rocks, there are Lick Branches in eleven Missouri counties, Lick Forks in three and Lick Creeks in thirteen.

Lick Creek (Marion). Fed by three springs of salt, sulphurs and magnesia which boiled up into pools, this creek was named for its deer licks (RF).

Licking (Texas). First called The Lick (RF), this town was named for a buffalo salt lick (VR). P.O. 1847-1863, 1866-now. Pop. 1,328.

Lickskillet (Cass, Grundy, Polk, Jackson, Harrison and others). Over the years, this favorite pioneer town name has fostered many stories. They'll say, for example, that the name came about because the storekeeper sold molasses by the skilletful, pouring it into the customer's jug and then put-

ting the skillet down for the dog to lick clean for the next customer. Or that the storekeeper's wife put her skillets out for the wolves to lick clean. In reality, the humorous name probably refers to the bad manners or poverty of some hapless early family, or it may have been a way the residents joked about themselves. All of the old Lickskillets went out of existence or changed their names (RF). See Mapleton, Pleasant Hope.

Liege [LEEJ] (Montgomery). First known as New Bellflower, for its neighbor Bellflower, the town was renamed for the capital of Belgium after soldiers came home from WWI. It is now part of Bellflower (LI). P.O. 1918-1954.

Lillard County. See Lafayette County.

Lincoln County [LING kuhn]. This county was not named for the president. It was named by an early citizen, who argued, "I was born, sir, in Lincoln County, North Carolina. I lived for many years in Lincoln County, in old Kentucky. I wish to live the remainder of my days and die in Lincoln County, in Missouri" (VR). Organized 1818. Pop. 28,892.

Lincoln School. Missouri has at least 18 schools named after Abraham Lincoln. Most of these were built for African American populations (RF).

Lincoln University (Cole). When peace came after the Civil War, a group of African American soldiers gave their pay to start a school to train newly freed black men as teachers. Lincoln Institute was set up in a log cabin in 1866 (LI).

Linn
Livingston County

Linn (Osage) county seat. The town was originally named Linnville, but the name was shortened. The name honors Democratic U.S. Senator Lewis F. Linn (VR). Home of the <u>Unterrified Democrat</u>, a newspaper which was named during the Civil War. Its editor declared he would remain "unterrified" no matter what threats he received (Enc). See also Linn County. P.O. 1844-now. Pop. 1,148.

Linn County [LIN]. Before county organization, this territory was known as Locust Creek Country, a hunting ground for settlers in Howard and Chariton Counties (LI). It was named for Lewis Fields Linn, a Democrat and supporter of Andrew Jackson, who had a long and colorful career in public office. As a U.S. senator (1833-1843), he was instrumental in bringing the Platte Purchase area into the state. He also wrote the bill to promote settlement in Oregon territory, earning himself the nickname "the Father of Oregon" (DM). See Oregon Trail. Organized 1837. Pop. 13,885.

Linneus [LIN ee uhs] (Linn) county seat. This name was originally Linnville, honoring Senator Lewis F. Linn (see Linn County). It was changed to Linneus. One source says the change was suggested by Senator Linn (DE). Another says the change was suggested by a lawyer who wanted the town to be named for Swedish botanist Karl Von Linne, commonly called Linnaeus. Although the lawyer threw a fit over the misspelling, people still misspelled it anyway (RF). P.O. 1840-now. Pop. 364.

Little Dixie. This central region of Missouri counties was settled by pioneers from the South, many of whom maintained their southern allegiance during the Civil War. Described in verse by Albert E. Trombley:

> It's the heart of Missouri, blooded of three,
> Virginia, Kentucky and Tennessee.
> It's a tall spare man on a blue-grass hoss.
> It's a sugar-cured ham without raisin sauce.
> It's coon dog, coon, persimmon tree.
> It's son or brother named Robert E. Lee . . .

Livingston County [LIV ing stuhn]. Named for Edward Livingston, the 11th secretary of state, who served in Andrew Jackson's cabinet two years (1831-1833) (RF). Organized 1837. Pop. 14,592.

Lizzie's (or Lizz's) Cut (St. Francois). The M.R. and B.T. Railroad cut through a hill here, creating a locally famous spot named for a woman who lived on the hill.

Low Wassie Creek [loh WAH see]. P.O. (Oregon) 1857-1867, 1871-1875, (Shannon) 1891-1943. See Hi Wassie.

Lone Jack (Jackson). A single blackjack tree marked the location of a spring on this prairie site. Today, there is a marble monument where Confederate soldiers were killed by Union forces. Union dead from this raid are buried in Leavenworth, Kansas. P.O. 1966-now. Pop. 392.

Long Branch. This popular creek name appears in fourteen Missouri counties. Usually, the name describes the length of a creek, or branch. Sometimes, it is named for a family living there (LI). A town in Monroe County bore the name. P.O. 1838-1850, 1856-1861, 1863-1865, 1867-1907.

Longview Park (Ray). This park with its grand house and barns was once the estate of R.A. Long, who made his money in lumber. The farm specialized in flowers, dairy, hogs and horses. Daughter Lula Long Combs, a horse lover, pushed for development of the Kansas City Royal into a stock and horse show of international renown (VR).

Loose Creek (Osage). The town is named for the creek, called L'Ours Creek by the French, "the bear creek." Americans pronounced the name Loose Creek because they didn't know French, and the name "loose" was fitting for a waterway that flooded the countryside every spring (RF). A priest for the Roman Catholic diocese of Jefferson City says that the origin is a corruption of "Louis, the French king" (LI). P.O. 1849-now. Pop. 300.

Lost Creek. Legend has it that an early settler got lost while hunting here and was eaten by a bear (CG).

Louisiana [luh wee zee AN uh] or [loo ee zee AN uh] (Pike). In 1804, Louisiana Basye was born in St. Louis. Her family named her for the Louisiana Purchase, Thomas Jefferson's purchase of all land west of the Mississippi. In 1818, when the Basyes moved to Pike County, their new hometown honored the child by using her name (RF). P.O. 1820-now. Pop. 3,967.

Loutre River
Lupus

Loutre River [LOO tuhr]. It would seem appropriate for the French to name a waterway for a common animal—otter. Other explanations have been given; writing the word *l'outre*, as it occasionally appears, changes its meaning to "the outer" or "utmost" (CG). This suggests that the name was perhaps given in comparison to another waterway (LI).

Lover's Leap. There are at least seven of these in Missouri. Most are complete with a legend involving two handsome young lovers, Native American or pioneer or a combination of the two. The tale is told that the lovers, rather than give up their love, jumped or were chased off the cliff and killed on the rocks below (LI).

Lupus [LOO puhs] (Moniteau). Two choices: This was first called Wolf's Point for the animal, (Enc), OR, it was first called Wolfe Point for John B. Wolfe, an early merchant (CG). The name was changed to the Latin word for "wolf" because another town had already claimed Wolf's Point. P.O. 1884-1955. Pop. 39.

M

Macedonia (Phelps). This post office was named for Macedonia, the region of Greece that was a Greek and then a Roman province. The apostle Paul began his missionary work in Macedonia (Acts 16:9) and thus it is the part of Europe believed to have received Christianity first. There are numerous Protestant churches and schools named Macedonia in Missouri (RF). P.O. 1890-1917.

Machens [MAH kuhnz] (St. Charles). This river town was first settled in the late 1700s by a family called Payne. Henry Ernst Machen and his family came here in 1848, and worked to bring the railroad through. Called Texas Junction, the town was later renamed for the family (LI). Much later, Charles Lindbergh gave folks something to talk about when his plane ran out of gas and landed here (LI). P.O. 1895-1956.

Charles Lindbergh once ran out of gas and landed in Machens.

Mackey (Dunklin). A Frisco Railroad flag stop established in 1920, it was named for a large landowner, Virgil McKay. The railroad spelled the name as it was pronounced rather than McKay as written (RF).

Macks Creek (Camden). The town was settled in the 1840s and named for the creek, the creek in turn was named for an early settler named Mack (RF). Today, it is well known to motorists as the place where you must drive the speed limit. P.O. 1872-now. Pop. 272.

Mackville (Lincoln). Named for Dr. McElwell, known as Mack. The 1899 atlas misspelled it Markville when published, and people still occasionally use the "r" spelling (RF). P.O. 1866-1904.

Macon County [MAY kuhn]. Named for Nathaniel Macon of North Carolina. One of his favorite sayings was, "If left alone, they will always do what's right," referring to the people (RF). Organized 1837. Pop. 15,345.

Macon (Macon) county seat. See Macon County. Two towns, Macon and Hudson, were combined as Macon City when the railroad came through in 1859 (VR). In 1862, Federal militia General Lewis Merrill ordered county seat Bloomington burned to drive out the families of southern sympathizers living there. However, one of Merrill's staff found a way to replace Bloomington without levelling it: he wrote a bill changing the county seat to Macon City. The word "City" was dropped in 1863. Nicknamed "The City of Maples," the courthouse stands in the midst of old trees given by a taxpayer in lieu of taxes (LI). P.O. 1856-now. Pop. 5,571.

Madison [MAD uh sn] (Monroe). Named for the fourth U.S. president, James Madison (see Madison County), this town was settled by Kentuckians who made their livings by shipping livestock and poultry. Fame came to Madison for its saddle horses, also called plantation horses, and trotters (VR). P.O. 1837-now. Pop. 518.

Madison County. Named for President James Madison (1751-1836), the president who declared war with England in 1812 (RF), this county boasts some of the oldest European-style settlements in Missouri. It was populated in the early days by French mine operators and African American slaves. Organized 1818. Pop. 11,127.

Madisonville (Ralls). NOT named for the president, but named for one of the president's namesakes, this rural hamlet was named for James Madison Crosthwaite by his half-brother, Jeptha Shelton Crosthwaite. Maps spelled the name Madison Ville until 1885 (RF). P.O. 1838-1906.

Magic Mountain (Taney). Historically known as Baird Mountain, in 1930 promoters changed the name as a way to advertise for customers touring this resort area.

Magneola Springs (St. Clair). First named Looney's Springs and Salt Creek Springs, the name was coined by Mrs. C.A. Mitchell in 1911, who believed the word, created from Latin, meant "great well" (RF).

Magnet (Atchison). One of Missouri's best promotional names, this was supposed to draw people, but the little town only lasted about 30 years (RF). P.O. 1880-1900.

Magnolia. Even though our unpredictable springs often spoil its blossoms, this southern plant has been popular in Missouri. The name, and the plant, came north with settlers, and was used by post offices in Clinton County (1853-1855) and Moniteau (1868-1875) and Johnson (1896-1953).

Maine Orchard (Taney). Now part of Hollister, Maine Orchard took its name from a clubhouse bought by a group of St. Louis gentlemen; the building was the State of Maine Building at the Louisiana Purchase Exposition of 1904, moved and rebuilt near a large peach orchard (RF).

Malden (Dunklin). A railroad town established in 1877 in the cotton country of southeast Missouri, the first buildings were those moved from the nearby hamlet of Cotton Hill (1850). (1) It was named for landowner Colonel T.H. Maulden. (2) It was named for Malden, Massachusetts, the hometown of one of the founders. Both explanations have supporters. P.O. 1877-now. Pop. 5,123.

Mallard (Henry). This was a railroad stop where members of the Kansas City Hunting Club—duck hunters—got off the train (RF).

Malta Bend (Saline). Even though most landmarks were named by the time the steamboat came along, there are a few place names from steamboat days. This is a bend in the Missouri River where the steamboat *Malta*, loaded with furs, struck a snag and sank. The town took the name from the bend (VR). P.O. 1860-1861, 1866-now. Pop. 289.

Manchester
Marais des Cygnes River

Manchester (St. Louis). The first settler in 1800 was Bryson O'Hare, who may have been a Native American from the East. Soon after, a settler named Jesse Hoard renamed it Hoardstown and finally an Englishman settled there and renamed it for his home place in England. The spot was renowned for its fine pastures and abundance of clear, spring water (RF). P.O. 1824-1902, 1904-1963. Pop. 6,482.

Manchester Road. This road from St. Louis to Manchester was laid out in 1835 and made a state road in 1839. It became the "Road to Jefferson City" and today is U.S. 50 (RF).

Manila (Pettis). Named for the capital city of the Philippine Islands and established soon after the Spanish-American War of 1898, the word *manila* comes from the Tagalog language and means a place where there are many nilads (flowering shrub with white blossoms, *Ixora Manila*) (RF). P.O. 1898-1904.

Mansfield (Wright). Laura Ingalls Wilder, who wrote the <u>Little House on the Prairie</u> books, lived and wrote here, but it was her daughter Rose Wilder Lane who made the town famous in her classic <u>The Old Home Town</u> (VR). The town is named for one of its developers. P.O. 1882-now. Pop. 1,429.

Map (Shannon). This was named by the first postmaster, Smith Martin, who looked for a short name that was unique (RF). P.O. 1917-1936.

Maple Sink (Oregon). This large sinkhole covers 10 acres, is 25 feet deep and covered with maple trees (RF).

Mapleton (Putnam). This small settlement was formerly known as Lick Skillet, but a more polite name was chosen for the post office. Maple names are one of our state's most popular categories, although there are more "oak" names by far (RF). P.O. 1891-1909.

Marais des Cygnes River [MER duh zeen]. French for "Marsh of the Swans" (VR), the story is as follows: The handsome brave, Coman of the Plains people, courted and won the love of Princess Osa of the Osage. Her grandfather, Chief White Hair, objected, but Osa was determined. When Coman came in his canoe, Osa loaded her luggage and stepped in. Here accounts vary. Did a flood overcome the craft? Did a terrible thing from below sweep the lovers under? No matter which version you believe, the canoe disappeared in great confusion. Miraculously, a pair of swans appeared on the water in its place, and swam gracefully and peacefully away. Every spring the two swans returned—watched for and reported on by excited Osage children (LI).

Marble Hill (Bollinger) county seat. This interesting name has two possible sources: At the time of its naming, there was a mistaken belief that the hill on which the town was built was marble (actually it's limestone). Another possibility: The tops of the nearby hills are rounded like marbles. Nearby Turkey Hill is shaped like a turkey (RF). P.O. 1868-now. Pop. 1,447.

Marceline [mahr suh LEEN] (Linn) county seat. This railroad town was named for Marcelina, the wife of a railroad official. This was the hometown of Walt Disney's family while Walt was a child, and Disneyland's Main Street is based on the town plan. P.O. 1887-now. Pop. 2,645.

March (Dallas). Named by postmaster T.C. Bennett for the month the post office was organized. In the 1930s it was nicknamed *Dogtown* because of the number of dogs around the settlement (RF). P.O. 1888-1915.

Maries County [MAIR iz]. Named for the two waterways which head in the county, the Maries River and the Little Maries. See Maries River. Organized 1855. Pop. 7,976.

Maries River. Occasionally said to be named after two local girls, both named Mary, it is more likely this name comes from *marais*, or "swamp" in French. It was probably named by early French explorers and trappers (RF). A priest from the Roman Catholic diocese of Jefferson City suggests that the origin is "the French name for the Virgin Mary" (LI).

Marion [MAHR ee uhn] (Cole). Founded in 1820, this town was named for General Francis Marion (RF). See Marion County. P.O. 1823-1953.

Marion City (Marion). This town was named for the county (see Marion County). Marion City was promoted to buyers as "the metropolis of the west," a prosperous finished community. Maps showed streets, banks, hotels and even a theatre and newspaper office. A few buildings were built, but the site was mostly abandoned after flooding in 1836 and the 1840s and 1850s. (VR). It has also been called Mystic City of Missouri (RF).

Marion County
Marrowbone Creek

Mark Twain called it "the City of Napoleon" in his <u>Gilded Age</u>. Charles Dickens called it "Eden" in his book <u>Martin Chuzzlewit</u>. P.O. 1837-1861.

Marion County. Early settlers from Virginia and Kentucky, many of whom were Revolutionary War veterans, named the town (first called Two Rivers Country) for General Francis Marion (1732-1745) of South Carolina. Known as the "Swamp Fox," he was renowned for his military genius in fighting for American independence against British forces. No other Revolutionary War hero other than George Washington has as many American places named in his honor. Another possible source: Marion County may be named for a county in Kentucky, home of many early settlers (RF). Organized 1826. Pop. 27,682.

Marionville (Lawrence). Named for General Francis Marion (see Marion County) this town is known for its population of white squirrels (LI). P.O. 1864-now. Pop. 1,920.

Mark Twain Cave (Marion). Now a popular tourist site, this cave was called Sims' Cave after its discoverer, who found it while chasing a cougar or panther (BH). It was later called McDowell's by local people, and McDougal's Cave in <u>Tom Sawyer</u>.

Mark Twain Lake. Near Mark Twain's boyhood home, this is Missouri's newest major lake for recreational boating and fishing. It was formed with the construction of the Clarence Cannon Dam. A state park here preserves the two-room cabin in which Samuel Clemens was born.

Marrowbone Creek (Daviess). According to oral tradition documented in 1929, "A party of venison and honey hunters killed six elk and roasted the bones for the marrow. All became ill from eating too much marrow." The same diners also named Dog Creek because "they had too much dog, too" (RF).

Marshall (Saline) county seat. This was named for the Chief Justice of the Supreme Court, John Marshall of Virginia, who died shortly before the town was incorporated (RF). P.O. 1840-now. Pop. 12,711.

Marshfield (Webster). Founders named this town in Webster County for the home of Daniel Webster in Marshfield, Massachusetts (VR). P.O. 1856-now. Pop. 4,374.

Marthasville (Warren). Founded by Dr. John Young, Benjamin Young and Aaron Young, the town was named for John Young's wife (VR). P.O. 1818-now. Pop. 674.

Martinsburg (Audrain). This town was laid out by William R. Martin, a native of Kentucky. P.O. 1870-now. Pop. 337.

Marvel Cave (Stone). Now a popular tourist cave, this was first explored in the mid-19th century and named Marble Cave for its marble. The marble operation never became profitable, but owners found a market for the bat manure, or guano, they found.

Maryland Heights (St. Louis). A railroad town on the old Chicago, Rhode Island and Pacific Railroad and now within the metro St. Louis region, this was named for the state of Maryland (RF). P.O. 1925-1960. Pop. 2,540.

Maryville (Nodaway) county seat. Named for Mary Graham, the wife of a powerful politician, this town later found fame as the birthplace of Dale Carnegie who wrote How to Win Friends and Influence People (RF). P.O. 1846-now. Pop. 10,663.

Mashek [MAH shuhk] (Lincoln). This Bohemian Catholic settlement was named for John Mashek, immigrant blacksmith who organized the first church services. It's now part of Hawk Point (RF). P.O. 1888-1905.

Mastodon State Park (Jefferson). Excavation of mastodon remains and Indian artifacts make this park one of North America's most important sites for study of Ice Age (12,000 B.C.) men and animals. See illustration next page.

Matson (St. Charles). The area around Matson was originally settled by Daniel Boone and Daniel Morgan Boone in the early 1800s. Among the

Maud
McBaine

first settlers from Kentucky was Abraham Shobe. In 1819, he bought the Boone claims. When Shobe died in 1838, his grandson Abraham Matson bought the claims (BD). In 1892, the Missouri-Kansas-Texas Railroad came through Matson. Richard Matson was instrumental in persuading the MK&T to build a station, water tank and coal chute in town in exchange for part of his land for a right-of-way.

Mastodon State Park is one of America's most important sites for Ice Age research.

Maud (Shelby). Originally called Black Hawk for the popular brand of bitters served there. Later called Stivers Corners (1869), then Petersburg, then Maud. The name was selected by the postmaster to honor his four-year-old daughter (RF). P.O. 1880-1903.

May Apple (Laclede). The town was named for the spring plant (RF), which is beautiful and abundant and bears a fruit which is usually eaten by raccoons before people can get to it. P.O. 1857-1859.

Mayflower (Barry). This was the only town in Missouri named for a Pilgrims' ship (RF). P.O. 1887-1910.

Maysville (DeKalb) county seat. This town may have been named for Maysville, Kentucky, though the original founders were from east Tennessee (RF). Its handsome courthouse is a monument to government thrift: Funds were too limited to build the structure of stone, so brick was ordered and stone used only for trim (MO). P.O. 1846-now. Pop. 1,176.

Mayview (Lafayette). This town was established on the site of an older community called Mounds, Heth's Hills or Heth's Knobs. The new name came from history-loving citizens who chose the name of an important site from the War of 1812. P.O. 1865-now. Pop. 279.

McBaine (Boone). This town was named in honor of Turner McBaine, who owned the town site's land (RF). In September of 1899, the first locomotive reached Columbia on the MK&T rail line that connected to the Katy here in McBaine. Turner McBaine realized the economic potential of this junction point, plotted the town of McBaine and auctioned off lots on September 20, 1899, only two weeks after the branch began operation. But the railroad saw McBaine as merely a convenient switching station. Passengers could hop on a train in Columbia at night, sleep until their car was switched to the eastbound Katy Flyer in McBaine and greet the morning in St. Louis without waking. P.O. 1894-1958. Pop. 6 people and 6 dogs (LI).

McDonald County [muhk DAH nld]. First called Snake County, this was renamed for a South Carolina soldier in the Revolutionary War (RF). Folklorist and writer Vance Randolph lived here during the 1930s and recorded and published an extensive and interesting collection about Ozark life (DM). Organized 1849. Pop. 16,938.

McMullin (Randolph). A coal-mining settlement named for the local store owner; this was first called Camp (RF). P.O. (Scott) 1880-1889, (Randolph) 1903-1924.

Meadville (Linn). This was first called New Baltimore (1860) and then Bottsville (1866) by storekeeper John Botts. Botts moved away in 1867 and the name was changed to Meadville to honor Charles Mead, superintendent of the Hannibal and St. Joe Railroad (RF). P.O. 1869-now. Pop. 360.

Mecca (Clinton). This village was probably named to signify that it was the goal of a pilgrimage (RF). P.O. 1898-1912.

Mechanicsburg (Macon). This small town was probably named by Ohioans who brought the name from their old state (RF).

Memphis [MEM fis] (Scotland) county seat. There was a post office called Memphis on the North Fabius River; a commission chose the spot for a county seat and took the name. This name was that of the earliest capital of Egypt, suggesting that founders studied the classics and tried to give significance to this wilderness village (RF). It fits in with other classical names in north Missouri. See Antioch, Hannibal. P.O. 1838-now. Pop. 2,094 .

Mendon (Chariton). Named for the Illinois home of the founder (RF). Near Swan Lake National Wildlife Refuge, this town is a favorite spot for duck and goose hunting in the fall (LI). P.O. 1872-now. Pop. 207.

Meramec River
Miami

Meramec River [MER uh mak] or [MER uh mek]. (1) The name sounds similar to the Chippewa *manumaig*, or catfish. It was picked up by the French and written several ways before being standardized (JL). (2) In 1700, Father Gravier wrote in his journal "We discovered the River Miaramegoua, where the very rich lead mine is situated" (VR). The river name was taken up by an ironworks (now a historic site) and towns in Phelps and Crawford Counties that spell the name in various ways. The river is a tributary of the Mississippi River.

Meramec State Park (Franklin). This 7,124 acres was purchased for a state park in 1928, and named for the Meramec River. The park contains more than 20 caves and is the site of a Civilian Conservation Corps camp.

Mercer County [MUHR suhr]. This was named for General Hugh Mercer who fought in the Battle of Princeton in 1777, at which the British were defeated. (The county seat is Princeton) (VR). Organized 1845. Pop. 3,723.

Merchants Bridge (St. Louis City). In the late 1880s, merchandise was sent to East St. Louis in Illinois, then brought over the Eads Bridge at an additional charge to St. Louis merchants. They objected, and this railroad bridge was built so freight could be shipped directly. The bridge opened in 1890.

Meta [MEE tuh] (Osage). Like many Missouri towns, this one is named for a lady—the sister of an early entrepreneur. There is a story, however, that she earned the naming in this way: One day, when she was chopping wood, she cut the tip of a finger off. The doctor sewed it back on, promising that if the finger grew back the town would be named after her. It did, and it was. P.O. 1903-now. Pop. 249.

Mexico [MEX sih ko] (Audrain) county seat. Folks here call themselves Mexicoans, to distinguish themselves from citizens of our neighboring nation. The town was named in recognition of the excitement over the Mexican War (RF). P.O. 1837-now. Pop. 11,290.

Miami [meye AM uh] (Saline). Platted as Greenville in 1838, it was re-named in 1853. (1) The name remembers a group of Miami Indians who established a village there around 1810 (VR). (2) It is a Chippewa word for "People who live on the peninsula" (JL). P.O. 1838-now. Pop. 142.

Midco
Mill Creek

Midco (Carter). A factory town for Kansas City's Mid Continent Iron Company, the population here swelled to 3,000 during World War I. An iron furnace and a charcoal furnace were the principle places of employment. The town had schools, a hotel and railroad. After the war, it fell to ruins (RF).

Middlebrook (Iron). Although there may be other reasons for the name, most likely it arose because the settlement was between Pilot Knob and Iron Mountain, two iron-mining towns (RF).

Middlegrove (Monroe). The name, originally two words, reflects the community's central location between the Mississippi and Missouri Rivers and the river port towns of New London and Franklin. It was a convenient stopping-off place for westward travelers and settlers in the mid-19th century. P.O. 1829-1907.

Middletown (Montgomery). This crossroads town is at the intersection of north-south and east-west roads. It is also in the middle of good farming country (RF). P.O. 1832-1835, 1837-now. Pop. 217.

Midway (Boone). This settlement is midpoint between Columbia and Rocheport on the historic Boonslick Trail and is today about half-way between St. Louis and Kansas City on Interstate 70. There have been Midways in Barton, Cooper, Newton, Putnam and Moniteau Counties. P.O. 1869-1908.

Milan [MEYE luhn] (Sullivan) county seat. Surveyed in 1845 by Wilson Baldridge, this town was probably named for Milan (Milano), Italy. The pronunciation is pure Missouri. P.O. 1847-now. Pop. 1,767.

Mildred (Taney). This town was named for the postmaster's youngest daughter (RF). P.O. 1910-1934.

Milford (Barton). This town was platted and named by Charles Milford Wilcox. There have been other Missouri Milfords: Johnson County (P.O. 1855-1863); Scotland County (P.O. 1841-1850) (RF). P.O. 1869-now. Pop. 22.

Mill Creek. There are 31 Mill Creeks in Missouri, along with four Mill Branches and other sites (townships, churches, schools, roads, prairies, springs, groves and hollows). Like the various places with "miller" in their names, these reflect the great importance in early days of having a mill in the community (RF).

Miller County
Mineola

Miller County [MIL uhr]. Established out of Cole County in 1837, this was named for John Miller, Missouri's fourth governor (1826-1832); Miller was an officer under General Benjamin Harrison in the War of 1812 and a member of Congress from Missouri from 1826-1842 (RF). In this county is the geographical center of Missouri. Organized 1837. Pop. 20,700.

Millersburg (Callaway). Laid out by Thomas Miller in 1829 and named for his former home of Millersburg, Kentucky. There were also Millersburgs in Franklin, Putnam and Shelby Counties. P.O. 1830-1953.

Milo [MEYE loh] (Vernon). This town was named for Milo Main, an elderly resident (RF). P.O. 1883-now. Pop. 76.

Milton (Randolph). See Firth. P.O. 1840-1872.

Mina Sauk Falls (Iron). Legend says Missouri's most impressive waterfall (105-foot drop) is named for the daughter of a Piankishaw chief who married an Osage warrior. The chief's advisors, declaring the girl bewitched, said that the warrior would have to die. They threw him from Taum Sauk Mountain. Mina Sauk leaped after. Lightning flashed and the side of the mountain opened; it was the birth of the beautiful Mina Sauk falls (VR).

Mindenmines (Barton). Probably named by German immigrants from Minden. It was Minden Mines until the government ordered all post offices to be one word for simplicity's sake (GS). P.O. 1884-now. Pop. 346.

Mine A Breton (Washington). Francois Azor was born in Brittany, France, and nicknamed "Breton." He is credited with finding the first lead here, in 1773. This town, which was further developed by Moses and Stephen Austin, was county seat until Potosi was founded. P.O. 1811-1824.

Mine la Motte [MEYEN luh MAHT] or [MEYEN luh MOHT] (Madison). The lead mines—and their consequent town—were founded by Antoine de la Mothe Cadillac, a French explorer in 1714. P.O. 1840-1861, 1867-now. Pop. 120.

Mineola [min ee OH luh] (Montgomery). Named for a supposedly Indian word meaning "healing water," this town is situated on the site of the earlier settlement of Loutre Lick (RF). A mineral spring gives it the name. The nearby Mineola Hill is the steepest Interstate 70 grade in Missouri. P.O. 1881-1967.

Mineral Springs (Barry). The first name of this resort was Panacea, Latin, meaning "supposed to cure all diseases." The name was changed to describe the springs more exactly. P.O. 1880-1895.

Mingo [MING goh] (Stoddard). Called Grindle at first (1846), the name was changed to Mingo, to echo Mingo Swamp, or Mingo Bottoms, the name of this region from its early days. Mingo was the name of Chief Paye Mmongo of the Chiacha tribe whose people lived in this region until 1834 (RF). A second opinion: The Delaware, who had been evicted from their eastern woodland homes, called all Iroquois people *mengwe* meaning "treacherous, stealthy" (JL). P.O. 1899-1905, 1909-1952.

Minimum (Iron). Named for postmaster N.A. Farr's wife, Minnie (RF).

Mirabile (Caldwell). At first called Marguam's Store (for William Marguam), the name was changed to reflect the nature of the place. *Mirabilis* in Latin means "wonderful" (RF). P.O. 1849-1941.

"Misere" (Ste. Genevieve). This early nickname for Ste. Genevieve means "misery." The settlers lived in tents or small cabins with little protection from the weather. They had to make, find or grow everything they needed. Life was hard, and even miserable.

Mississippi County
Missouri River

Mississippi County [mis uh SIP ee]. This county was named, by act of the legislature, for the river. Its brick courthouse, designed by Jerome B. Legg, is the same as that of St. Charles, but the St. Charles version is made of gray stone (MO). Organized 1845. Pop. 14,442.

Mississippi River. Called by DeSoto *Rio Grande del Espirite Santo* (the grand river of the holy spirit), called by Marquette *Riviere de la Conception* (River of the holy conception) in fulfillment of a vow he made to the Virgin Mary, called by Robert de La Salle *Riviere Colbert* in honor of a French minister, called by French trappers *Riviere de St. Louis*, in honor of the patron saint of their king (see St. Louis), it is the Native American word that stuck. A few experts have tried to construct it thusly: *Missi*, meaning "great" and s*eepee*, meaning "river" (LI). Most likely it meant "Big River," one of the river's nicknames today (RF). Another nickname is "Father of Waters," popularized by Henry Wadsworth Longfellow in the ballad *Evangeline*. The poet describes:
   . . . the lands where the Father of Waters
Siezes the hills in his hands, and drags them down to the ocean . . .

Missouri City (Clay). In 1859, three towns were combined and incorporated under the name Missouri City, for the state. The three combined towns were: (1) Richfield, named for the son of the town's tavern owner; (2) Atchison, named for the Democratic U.S. senator from Missouri 1843-1855; and (3) St. Bernard, named for the famous alpine pass (RF). P.O. 1867-now. Pop. 348.

Missouri Half-Breed Tract (Clark). This land was part of the Sac and Fox hunting tribes and named for a half-breed woman who once owned it. Her name was Kataiqua (LI).

"Missouri Rhineland." This is a nickname for the region of bluffs along the Missouri River between St. Louis and Jefferson City. This name recalls a beautiful part of Germany along the Rhine River (LI).

Missouri River [muh ZOO ruh] or [muh ZOO ree] or [mi ZOO ree]. One river historian says that the Missouri River should be considered the main river and the Mississippi its tributary, making the Missouri the longest river in the United States. However, European explorers traveled on the Mississippi first, then discovered the Missouri, and this established the Mississippi as the main river. The origin of the place name is also debatable: A reliable modern authority says it's a French copy of a Native American word. The French heard it from their Illinois guides, who used it to refer to the people who lived on the river (LI). The Illinois tribes called these people "Missouri," or "People of the Big Canoes" because of the Missouri tribe's large canoes, which were dug out from giant cottonwood trees. The people's name for themselves was something that sounded like "Ne-o-eta-cha" or "Ne-o-ge-he" (DE), also written Niutachi, which may have meant "People who dwell at the mouth of the river" (RF).

The French explorers Marquette and Joliet were the first white people to travel the Missouri River and write the name in their records.

How to pronounce Missouri

The experts agree that the word *Missouri* was first pronounced by Illinois Indian guides who traveled with Marquette and Joliet. The word, recorded by Marquette, referred to the people who lived here. He wrote it phonetically. Transferring it to simplified spelling, it was pronounced "oo eh meh soo REET" and means "where Missouris are."

After Marquette's journal, visitors recorded the word in several ways. It became the generally accepted name of the river. Some simply respelled it, others sounded it out as they heard it. So how is the word supposed to sound? The pronunciation has been in dispute throughout its lifetime.

"'Mizzoura' rolls from the tongue with melifinous [*sic*] grandeur. It must be spoken with open mouth and erect head," observed Boonville's <u>Weekly Advertiser</u> in 1897, "It suggests beauty and greatness. 'Mizzoury' is diminutive. It ends in a piping squeak. A lion's roar to the pewee's pipe! . . . a pretty name for a nice little school girl, but it will never do for the Queen of the Union."

In 1897, Walter Williams, founder of the MU School of Journalism, wrote about another pronunciation style: "Recently . . . there has sprung up in this state a preference for a pronunciation that gives the hissing sound of `s' to the letters and we hear, among our newly imported friends, that the name should be M-i-s-s-o-u-r-i. This is not euphonious; it is contrary to established usage; it is incorrect. It is a fad that should not be transplanted to our state."

Williams also asserted that "The old-fashioned said either Mizzourah or Mizzouri, the best educated the latter." His statement correctly acknowledges that pronunciation is partly a matter of fashion, and that each generation finds its own way. But Williams repeats the notion that the split between -ah and -ee has to do with schooling. Other thinkers have said that the split has to do with rural vs. urban dwellers or with southerners vs. northerners. None of these notions holds water.

The arguments were well practiced and oft repeated by the time Professor of English Donald Lance started his linguistic research in the state. In 1969 Lance began polling Missourians on their pronunciation of the name. His surveys are complex, breaking out preferences along the lines of age and length of residence. Among people born before 1945, he found a preference for the "uh" ending, but each generation since shows a greater preference for "ee." In most parts of the state, both pronunciations are traditional.

As far as "urban vs. rural," "educated vs. uneducated," or "southern vs. northern," Lance's findings dispute all these theories. Instead, he found a preference for "ee" in the eastern part of the state and "uh" in the west. Other scholars, polling people in the 1930s-1950s across the United States, found a preference for "-uh" in parts of the New England states of Vermont, Massachusetts, Connecticut, New Jersey and the southeastern states of West Virginia and North Carolina.

As time has gone on, the "uh" ending [muh ZOO ruh] is disappearing thanks to standardization in the media and the perception that "uh" is somehow hillbilly-ish. A survey at the state fair in 1989 recorded 1,942 people saying "Mizzouree" and 1,074 saying "Mizzouruh." It is interesting to observe, however, especially in an election year, how the old "uh" pronunciation rolls off the tongues of our politicians, evoking memories of the glorious linguistic past.

Missouri, The Bullion State
Missouri, The Puke State

Missouri, The Bullion State. This nickname for Missouri came about because of Senator Thomas Hart Benton, one of our first senators, who took a stand in favor of establishing a monetary standard based on gold and silver only. See Benton County.

Missouri, The Cave State. Missouri has 5,200 known caves, with 250 more being discovered every year. We also have 31 "show" caves, more than any other state.

Missouri, The Iron Mountain State. This nickname was given in the days when Iron Mountain was thought to consist entirely of iron.

Missouri, The Lead State. This early nickname was given to Missouri because of the productive lead mines in the southeastern part of the state.

Missouri, The Mule Capital of the World. The Missouri Mule was developed as a draft animal by 19th-century entrepreneurs in this state, who bred large jacks (male donkeys) with draft horse mares (females). At the Louisiana Exposition (1904), the Missouri Mule was a major attraction. "Mule Capital of the World" has been claimed by several Missouri towns and counties, including: Tarkio, which was famous for one breeder's fancy round brick barn; Smithton, the location of an important and award-winning mule breeder and raiser; Fulton, which was known for its huge mule auctions; and Warrensburg, with the largest mule dealer in the United States during World War I.

Missouri, The Outlaw State. Missouri earned this nickname after the Civil War, when Jesse James and other outlaw bands roamed the state, sometimes protected by sympathetic citizens.

Missouri, The Puke State. The origin for this unattractive nickname is unclear. It may have been given by folks associated with the Galena, Illinois, lead mines where so many Missouri miners had emigrated that it was said Missouri had taken a "puke." Another theory for the name is that it was given by Californians when Missourians moved west; Californians thought all the migrant Missourians came from Pike County, and corrupted the word. One source suggests that Missourians got so homesick when they left the state that they went around "pukin' and pinin'." Another suggests that settlers coming into the state on riverboats were so overjoyed to get off the boats and pick fresh greens that they overindulged, making themselves sick. Still another story tells that, while Illinois residents (who were called "suckers") learned to use straws to drink from scummy ponds, the Missourians just threw themselves down on the water and drank, then vomited. Whatever the origin, during the Civil War this nickname was used against Missouri's southerners by northern raiders (LI).

Missouri, The Show-Me State. The almost-official nickname, this slogan is identified worldwide with Missouri, appearing on our license plates, antique stores and barbecue sauce labels. Willard Duncan Vandiver is credited with originating the saying in 1899 when he was a member of the U.S. House of Representatives. He said, "I come from a state that raises corn and cotton and cockleburs and Democrats, and frothy eloquence neither convinces nor satisfies me. **I am from Missouri. You have to show me.**" Vandiver may have borrowed the phrase, however. Stories credit it to a Spanish-American War recruit from Missouri who served as a guard. He insisted on being shown passes, even from people he knew. Other sources suggest the phrase came from a song, or the words of a swaggering bully. Others credit bosses trying to teach jobs to young Missourians, such as a hotel manager tutoring an inept bellhop, or an exasperated Colorado mining boss trying to teach a Missouri miner the job. In this version, the boss finally says, "He's from Missouri; you have to show him." In 1912, Governor Hadley offered $500 for a more suitable expression to use for a state slogan, and many dignified phrases were offered but none have stuck.

Missouri Zion. Mormon Prophet Joseph Smith told hundreds of his followers that Missouri would be a haven after they were chased from Illinois. Zion, part of Jerusalem, is associated with the Promised Land.

Moark (Dunklin). This town is close to the border of Missouri and Arkansas (JL). P.O. 1900-1905.

Moberly [MOH buhr lee] (Randolph). This was named for Colonel William E. Moberly, first president of the Chariton and Randolph Railroad. When the ailroad hooked up with the North Missouri line, residents of nearby Allen were asked to move to the new junction. Only one Allen resident complied, but the town still sprang up, and was known as "The Magic City" because it grew overnight out of thin air. An 1867 advertising brochure for the North Missouri Railroad notes "In the east, the towns and cities make the railroads—here the railroads make the cities and towns." P.O. 1869-now. Pop. 12,839.

Moccasin Springs
Moniteau River

Moccasin Springs (Cape Girardeau). Probably named for poisonous water moccasins in the area, this certainly refers to the fact that the swampy land is only fit for snakes and other wild critters (RF). P.O. 1903-1909.

Moccasinville (Macon). When settlers first came here, they had no shoe leather so they made moccasins for their feet (APM).

Mokane [moh KAYN] (Callaway). As a Missouri River town, this was named Smith's Landing for a pioneer woman remembered today as Mrs. Smith. The town was washed away in a flood, rebuilt and named St. Aubert Landing (RF). Similarly named St. Aubert Station was across the river in Osage County, so that one riverboat captain remembered St. Aubert Landing on the left, St. Aubert Station on the right, and a ferry taking mail between the two (BH). Another flood forced the landing inland, to be renamed Mokane when the Missouri, Kansas and Texas Railroad came through and established a division headquarters in 1908. The headquarters left in the 1920s, and after a devastating flood in 1951, the town declined (RF). P.O. 1893-now. Pop. 186.

Monegaw Springs (St. Clair). The Osage Chief Monegaw retreated to a cave near here and starved himself to death, in sadness because his land was taken over by white settlers (DE). The spring was first called Stinking Waters because of its high sulphur content (RF).

Monett [MOH net] (Barry). Originally called Billings, then Plymouth Junction, it was surveyed by F.W. Bond in 1887 and renamed; Monett was the name of the General Passenger Agent for the New York Central Railway (APM). P.O. 1887-now. Pop. 6,529.

Moniteau County [MAH nuh toh] or [MAH nuh taw]. This county is named for the waterway that runs through it (RF). See Moniteau River. Organized 1845. Pop.12,298.

Moniteau River. This name is based on the Fox nation's word for the Deity, *manito* or *manitou* (RF). There is dispute whether the name means something like "creator" "great spirit" or "almighty." Earliest diaries and journals were written by Europeans, and the writers brought their own understanding to Native American words. We'll never know exactly what it meant to the early Native American (LI). Two post offices have been named for the river—one in Cole County (1830) and one in Moniteau (1882-1884).

Moniteau Creek
Montgomery City

Moniteau Creek. This creek flows into the Missouri River and divides Boone and Howard counties, near Rocheport. See Moniteau River.

Monitor Creek. This creek name is a variation of Moniteau.

Monkey Mountain (Holt). Two good stories here: One tells that a group of monkeys camped here after running away from a circus in nearby St. Joseph. The other theory is that the terrain is so steep only a monkey could get around (LI).

Monkey Run (Ralls). Some young men in town started trouble with some outsiders, and were chased home with the other boys yelling "Run, you Monkeys!" The town soon became known as the place where the "Monkey Runners" live. (LI).

Monroe City [muhn ROH] (Monroe). Platted in 1857 by E.B. Talcott as a shipping point for Missouri's first railroad, settlers from the South planted bluegrass and began the business of breeding horses and the pastime of foxhunting. It was known for its foxhounds and fine horses (VR). P.O. 1860-now. Pop. 2,701.

Monroe County. Missourians rushed to organize a state government so they could be recognized in time to vote in the 1820 presidential election. Even though the legality of Missouri's votes was questioned, their choice was elected, President James Monroe. Organized 1831. Pop. 9,104.

Montana (Iron). This post office existed in wild, unsettled land good for free-range cattle ranching, hence the name (RF).

Montauk [mahn TAWK] (Dent). This spring at the headwaters of the Current River, was the site of one of the first mills in the region. The mill spawned a village which was the county seat. Today it is a state park. The name is Native American. It may be a corruption of *minnawtawkit*, meaning "island place," or "spirit" or "spirit tree." The name was apparently used by Indian nations on the east coast, and its arrival here is a mystery (RF). It was a Missouri post office name from 1844-1974.

Montgomery City [mahnt GUHM uh ree] (Montgomery) county seat. This town was made the county seat in 1889 after much opposition from the residents in the southern part of the county. The town takes its name from the county (RF). P.O. 1857-now. Pop. 2,281.

Montgomery County. Three reasons are offered for the name: (1) It is named for General Richard Montgomery, a hero of the Revolutionary War; (2) it could be named for Montgomery County, Kentucky, because so many citizens of the county had settled here; (3) it was named for explorer Zebulon Montgomery Pike, the citizens being disappointed because Pike County had already taken his last name (RF). Organized 1818. Pop. 11,355.

Monticello [mahn tuh SEL oh] (Lewis) county seat. This town occupies a commanding position on the river bluffs, overlooking the fertile river valley and the hills that stretch away in all directions. Its name, which translates to "secret mountain" from the Latin, may be for its location. Its streets are named for famous men of the state and nation (RF). The name was given in honor of Thomas Jefferson's home (LI). P.O. 1834-now. Pop. 106.

Moon Lake (Vernon). This lake is named for its shape (RF).

Moon Town (St. Francois). Sometimes written as one word, this was a small lead-mining community named for the Moon family (RF).

Moral (McDonald). This was a small southwestern Ozarks town whose name was "possibly given for idealistic reasons" (RF). P.O. 1904-1908.

Moreau River [muh ROH] or [MAW roh] (Morgan, Moniteau, Cole). This is an early French name, first recorded as Riviere a Moreau. It was renamed Marrow Creek by the Lewis and Clark expedition, but the original French spelling continued to be used. One translation of the word from the French is "extremely black."

Morgan County [MAWR guhn]. Named for a revolutionary hero, General Daniel Morgan (1736-1802), "who displayed great bravery at the battle of Cowpens (1781) in the defeat of Tarleton" (RF). Morgan's name has been adopted by counties in eight other states. Organized 1833. Pop. 15,574.

Mormon Fork Creek. A tributary of the Grand River, this was named for the short-lived Mormon settlement there; the group was driven out of Jackson County in 1833 (RF). Locally known as Mormon Fork, as "fork" and "creek" are synonymous, this is one of the few places in Missouri with "Mormon" in its official name.

Mormon's Fork (Vernon). This short-lived post office was named for its creek (LI). See Mormon Fork Creek. P.O. 1852.

Morrison (Gasconade). Named for the owner of a large plantation before the Civil War, Alfred W. Morrison (RF). P.O. 1860-now. Pop. 160.

Morton (Ray). First known as Shaw's Shop due to the family who operated the community blacksmith shop, the name was changed to that of the local landowner (RF). P.O. 1874-1904.

Moscow (Clay). This was named for the Russian capital city through the influence of a Russian immigrant who kept the village one-room general store. Twenty other states have a Moscow and the name is considered by scholars to be a stock name in the United States (RF). P.O. 1874-1904.

Moscow Mills [MAH skow] (Lincoln). Near an important mill on the Cuivre River, this town was known as Moscow or Moscow on the Cuivre until people discovered there was already a Moscow in the state (Clay County) and needed to change the name (RF). P.O. 1878-now. Pop. 924.

Moselle [moh ZELL] (Franklin). This lead-mining community, established 1849, was called Moselle Iron Furnace. Iron ore was smelted and pig iron made here until 1874. The name comes from Moselle, France, a historic mining region and river in Lorraine (RF). P.O. 1860-1863, 1865-1871.

Mound City (Holt). Many schools, creeks and villages in Missouri are built on or near old Native American mounds. These mysterious man-made hills had value for the early people, and it was symbolic for Europeans and Americans to take them over. This town was named for a low mound where part of the town is built (VR). P.O. 1871-now. Pop. 1,273.

Mound City
Murder Rock

"Mound City" (St. Louis). This nickname for St. Louis referred to a giant Indian mound on the site when the city was founded. Little by little, the mound was hauled away (LI).

Mount Leonard (Saline). This name resulted from an engineer's drawing that made a ridge look like a mountain. Railroad designers, seeing the mountain, determined that the tracks would have to detour eight miles around it. The president of the line traveled to the site and commanded the engineers to follow him as he rode his horse straight up and over the ridge. The line was laid on his path and named Mount to commemorate the error and Leonard for the name of the farmer who owned the land (RF). Pop. 96.

Mount Nebo (Crawford). First called Jumping Off Place because of its steepness, the new name was taken from the Bible. Moses viewed the promised land from Mount Nebo (RF).

Mt. Vernon (Lawrence) county seat. This name, taken from the name of George Washington's home in Virginia, has been popular for seats of government. The name was earlier used for the temporary court site in Lafayette County (RF). P.O. 1837-now. Pop. 3,726.

Mountain Grove (Wright). The stores and post office of Hickory Springs knew their days were numbered when the railroad missed the town. So, they moved lock, stock and barrel to a new site, establishing Mountain Grove (VR). It was named for its location (LI). P.O. 1875-now. Pop. 4,182.

Mud Creek. At least nine Missouri creeks and branches have been named Mud and fourteen named Muddy; the Missouri River is well known as Big Muddy. "Too thick to drink and too thin to plow," the saying goes. One town (in Caldwell County) used Muddy as a name, probably because it was near one of the creeks. P.O. 1875-1877. Another used Muddy Fork (Knox) P.O. 1856-1859. Muddy Lane (Livingston) P.O. 1868-1901 had the longest existence of the muddy places. Mudville (Phelps) P.O. 1903-1905 seems to have had the most direct connection.

Murder Rock (Taney). Bandits hid behind this rock on the Harrison-Springfield Road, and waylaid travelers.

Napoleon (Lafayette). This Missouri River town was established in 1836 and named Poston's Landing after the storekeeper (CG). The town was also called Lisbon after the mayor's daughter (Elizabeth). But, like many other towns, the post office name was already chosen and the town changed its name to Napoleon (LI). The Emperor Napoleon had been important in Missouri history and was also a stock name in the United States (RF); the name is particularly appropriate for a town in Lafayette County, a county named after a French man. "Napoleon and Wellington met at Waterloo" is a popular local saying about the area towns names (LI). See Wellington and Waterloo. P.O. 1869-now. Pop. 233.

Nashville (Barton). This town was named by settlers for Nashville, Tennessee (RF). P.O. 1861-1863, 1867-1959.

Nashville (Boone). See Providence. P.O. 1820-1822, 1835-1844, 1846-1856.

Nation, The (Harrison). In this region, the grassy hills seem to go on forever. In "desperado days," say locals, you could be hidden here by sympathizers and the law would never find you (LI).

Naylor (Ripley). This small railroad town was first called Barfield, but freight was sometimes missent to Barfield, Arkansas. The name was changed to that of a land surveyor and Union Army captain from Indiana (RF). P.O. 1982-now. Pop. 642.

Needmore (Greene). According to legend, the store here was constantly out of some needed item or another. This was a popular pioneer name, used in at least four Missouri places (RF). P.O. 1890-1903.

Nemo (Hickory). Local informants told researchers the name means "little," and that it was given in response to the 1894 post office request that names be short and individual. But the name is a stock name, perhaps given for the hero of Jules Verne's <u>Twenty Thousand Leagues Under the Sea</u>, published in 1870 (RF). *Nemo* is Latin for "nobody." P.O. 1893-1896, 1899-1913.

Neosho [nee OH shoh] (Newton) county seat. Neosho is said to be a corruption of the Osage Indian word *neozho*, which means "clear, cold water"; the city is built around great springs (RF). P.O. 1839-now. Pop. 9,254.

Nevada [nuh VAY duh] (Vernon) county seat. First named Hog Eye, used to denote a sinkhole or depression in the earth, the settlement was renamed by its first permanent resident for Nevada City, California, after the Gold Rush (RF). *Nevada* is Spanish for "snowy," a common descriptive term for mountains, and the name of a mountain range in California. Later, a town in Texas was named after the one in Missouri (GS). Nicknamed during Civil War times as "Bushwhackers' Capital," it was burned to the ground by northern troops in 1863 (VR). P.O. 1856-1861, 1863, 1866-now. Pop. 8,597.

New Bloomfield (Callaway). First named Bloomfield, "New" was added when it was learned there was already a Bloomfield in existence (Enc). The name was a stock name, popular with settlers. P.O. 1841-now. Pop. 480.

New Cambria [NOO KAM briuh] (Macon). A railroad and coal-mining town originally named Stockton, this was renamed New Cambria to attract settlers of Welsh background to Missouri (APM). *Cambria* is the Latin word the Romans used to name the British Isles region they conquered, now known as Wales. P.O. 1864-now. Pop. 223.

New Florence (Montgomery). This town was named Florence for the daughter of the major landowner, but changed because there was already a Florence in Morgan County (RF). P.O. 1858-now. Pop. 801.

New Franklin (Howard). The current population of New Franklin depends on which way you come into town. One end says 1,107; the other 1,122. See Franklin.

New Hartford (Pike). This town was named for its township, and the township was named for the town in Connecticut and the town in Connecticut for the town in England (RF). P.O. 1871-now.

New Haven (Franklin). The earliest name and post office here was Blish's Mill, from a flour mill. Later, the name Miller's Landing (or Bend, Station, or -burg) was applied. New Haven was renamed when the town was laid out: It was a new town, and a haven for shipping. Often, the name was spelled as one word (RF). P.O. 1858-now. Pop. 1,757.

New Home (Bates). After the Civil War, Samuel Hawkins built a new house to replace one burned in the fighting. His wife named the place (APM). P.O. 1872-1902.

New London (Ralls) county seat. William Jameson, an Englishman, selected the site, saying he would build a town that would rival London (VR). P.O. 1820-now. Pop. 988.

New Madrid [nyoo MAD rid] (New Madrid). When he planned the city in 1789, New Jersey developer George Morgan settled on the name New City of Madrid to honor the Spanish king. At the time, the Spanish owned the territory and were attempting to close the Mississippi River to American traffic, and Morgan's Spanish city would have become the shipping point for traffic from the frontier to New Orleans. His plan set aside land for the king, for the Roman Catholic church and for Native American hunters. Although he did not see the plan through, a few settlers stayed. Their settlement was destroyed by floods and earthquake. It has, of course, been rebuilt in a better location (LI). See Greasy Cove. P.O. 1805-now. Pop. 3,350.

New Madrid handbill soliciting settlers:

R eal estate promoters have been part of the American scene since the earliest days. In 1788, George Morgan distributed this offering:

Several Gentlemen, who propose to make Settlements in the Western Country, mean to reconnoiter and survey the same the ensuing Winter. All Farmers, Tradesmen, &c. of good Characters, who wish to unite in this Scheme, and to visit the Country under my Direction, shall be provided with Boats and Provisions for the purpose, free of Expense, on signing an Agreement, which may be seen by applying to me . . .

The Boats which will be employed on this Expedition, are proposed to be from 40 to 60 Feet long, to row with twenty Oars each, and to carry a Number of Swivels. Each Man to provide himself with a good Firelock or Rifle, Ammunition, and one Blanket, or more if he pleases—Such as choose Tents, or other Convenience, must provide them for themselves.

Every Person who accompanies me in this Undertaking, shall be entitled to 320 Acres of Land at one eighth of a Dollar per Acre. Those who first engage to have the Preference of Surveys; which, however, each Person may make in such Part of the whole Tract as he pleases, taking none by his Choice of the best Lands; provided each Survey is either a Square or Oblong whose Sides are East, West, North and South; 640 Acres, or more, being first reserved for a Town, which I propose to divide into Lots of One Acre each, and give 600 of them, in Fee, to such Merchants, Tradesmen, &c. as may apply on the Spot, and 40 of them to such Public Uses as the Inhabitants may apply on the Spot and 40 of them to such Public Uses and the Inhabitants shall, from Time to Time, recommend; together with one Out Lot of 10 acres to each of the first 600 Families who shall build and settle in the Town.

continued

> All persons who settle with me at New-Madrid, and their Posterity, will have the free Navigation of the Mississippi, and a Market at New-Orleans, free from Duties, for all the Produce of their Lands, where they may receive Payment in Mexican dollars for their Flour, Tobacco, &c...
>
> School masters will be engaged immediately for the Instruction of Youth—Ministers of the Gospel will meet with Encouragement; and Grants of Land made in Fee to each of every Denomination, who may agree with a Congregation before the Year 1790 . . .
>
> Those who wish for further Information, will be pleased to apply to me in Person as above-mentioned, or at the New City of Madrid, after the first Day of next December, where Surveyors will attend to lay out the Lands.
>
> George Morgan
> October 3, 1788

New Madrid County. One of the first five counties, this was organized when Missouri was still a territory, and it was named for the existing town (see New Madrid). Organized 1812. Pop. 20,928.

New Melle [nyoo MEL ee] (St. Charles). This was named by settlers for a town, Melle, in Germany (RF). P.O. 1850-now. Pop. 486.

"New Thermopylae." In his book Martin Chuzzlewit, Charles Dickens used this name to poke fun at the pretentious names of American frontier towns. Promoted as an important landing, the heroes find that New Thermopylae is in reality "A steep bank with an hotel like a barn on the top of it; a wooden store or two; and a few scattered sheds." The name uses "new" in the self-important way of places named New York or New Jersey, minor spots compared to the European counterparts of Dickens' day. Thermopylae is the name of a mountain pass into Greece. It means, in Greek, "hot gates." The pass was made difficult by hot sulfur springs in the vicinity. At least two famous battles were fought at this pass and, eventually, reference to Thermopylae came to mean heroic resistance to hopeless circumstances. Dickens' town is the port (or gate) where his heroes hopefully disembark on their way to invade the disappointing Eden. The model for New Thermopylae was Hannibal. See Hannibal.

Newton County [NOO tn]. Named for John Newton, a Revolutionary War hero. Like William Jasper (see Jasper County), he was one of "Marion's Men" (see Marion County) (RF). Organized 1838. Pop. 44,445.

Niangua [neye ANG gwah] (Webster). This name is probably Sioux, with *ni* meaning "river" (GS). P.O. 1870-now. Pop. 459.

Niongwha River. This is a variant of Niangua.
Nirvana (Texas). The popular understanding is that this is the Buddhist word for that state of being when the soul is at one with God. Perhaps the name was given humorously, as this was a peaceful place (RF). P.O. 1891-1903.

Nishnabotna River [NISH nuh baht nuh] or [NISH uh] (Atchison). This is probably Sioux, with *ni* meaning "river" (GS). P.O. 1871-1953.

Niska River. A river with a Native American name that means "white river" (LI).

Nixa [NIK suh] (Christian). This unusual name may be a play on the name of an early settler, Nicholas Inman (APM). P.O. 1881-now. Pop. 4,893.

Nodaway County [NAH duh way]. This county was named for the principal waterway running through it. Organized 1845. Pop. 21,709.

Nodaway River. The meaning is in dispute. (1) Is it a corruption of *Nadowe-is-iw*, the Chippewa name for the Sioux, meaning "enemy" (VR)? (2) Does it mean "snakes," "aliens," "placid water" or "placid" (RF)? (3) Or is it a version of the Virginia name Nottaway, coming to Missouri with settlers (LI)? Washington Irving's <u>Astoria</u> is about a spring journey from this river (he calls it Naduet) up the Missouri (VR).

Noel [NOH uhl] (McDonald). Named for a prominent family, people often send mail to the Noel postmaster during the Christmas season to have the mail postmarked with this festive name (LI). P.O. 1886-now. Pop. 1,169.

Nonsuch (Camden). This post office was named the same as Henry VIII's old place in Surrey. The palace was built by the best Italian architects and landscapers, to make it exceptional, and the name echoes that idea (RF).

Normandy (St. Louis). Known as Little Rome for its many Catholic institutions, this town was founded by Charles Lucas. Lucas named the place for Normandy, France (RF). Lucas was killed in a duel with Thomas Hart Benton. P.O. 1857-1932. Pop. 5,025.

North River. This river flows northeast to empty into the Mississippi about ten miles north of Hannibal. It was first called the Jeffreon or Jeffrion. Many northeast Missouri names were changed after the War of 1812, when whites were mostly driven out of that area. When they returned, names of direction (North, South, East, Middle and West) were given to rivers and branches (LI).

Northmoor (Platte). This is a suburb of Kansas City with a name decidedly British, like many Missouri town names (RF). P.O. 1927-1947. Pop. 441.

Not (Shannon). Named for a large knot on the black oak that stood by its entrance, the first postmaster was NOT a speller (APM). P.O. 1886-1917.

Notch (Stone). This was the post office of Levi Morrill, known as Old Ike to readers of Harold Bell Wright's sentimental novel Shepherd of the Hills, published in 1907. The clearing was just a Notch in the road on the heavily wooded hillside (LI). P.O. 1895-1934.

Novelty (Knox). The eccentric store owner here stocked his business with a great variety of necessities, then put a flagpole in front so the place could be seen from far away. Was the town named for the novel merchandise or the novel flagpole? There are two schools of thought (LI). P.O. 1854-now. Pop. 143.

Novinger [NAH vin jurh] (Adair). The town is named for John C. Novinger, a developer (RF). P.O. 1879-now. Pop. 542.

O'Fallon (St. Charles). This town, now a commuter town for St. Louis business, was named for Major John O'Fallon, St. Louis capitalist and director of the North Missouri Railway (VR). P.O. 1820-now. Pop. 16,698.

Oak Grove (Franklin). The mighty oak, with its reputation for strength and endurance, has been chosen more often than any other tree to name Missouri places. Oak Grove is one of the few names that appears twice on the official highway map. This town is also called Oak Grove Village, to distinguish it from Oak Grove City. Pop. 4,565.

Oak Grove (Jackson). A name that appears in two places on the state highway map, this is sometimes distinguished from the other Oak Grove by using the complete name Oak Grove City. Oak is Missouri's most popular tree for place names. P.O. 1840-1862, 1867-now. Pop. 402.

Oakdale (Shelby). The first settlement in the county, this name was given by an early settler for the black oaks on a hill behind his home; it was written Oak Dale until around 1870 (RF).

Oakton (Barton). This town was first called Oak Grove, but the name was changed because Oak Grove City was already in use. P.O. 1897-1901.

Oasis (Taney). The first postmaster here changed the name from Cedar Valley, which is certainly descriptive of the place. Two ideas: Does Oasis describe the valley as a comfortable stopping place, or was the postmaster celebrating his new marriage as "an oasis in his life"? (RF).

Obrazo Creek. Probably named for a French family, Brazeau, and the "O" replaced *Aux*, meaning "at the place of" (GS).

Odd (Texas). Founder Ransom Lynch thought this town name was distinctive, but post office officials made him change it (RF). See Bucyrus.

Odessa [oh DESS uh] (Lafayette). First named Kirkpatrick for one of the founders, the honoree was certain that the town would fail and insisted that the name be changed. The president of the Chicago and Alton Railroad suggested Odessa, because the gently rolling fields reminded him of the country near the Russian town (Enc). P.O. 1874-now. Pop. 3,695.

Old Field Chute (Texas). When the Big Piney River washed a field away, it left the old coffins of an unmarked cemetery visible in the river bank (GA).

Old Mines (Washington). A French village founded in the 18th century at the site of important lead mines, this name compares these old, worked lead mines with Mine A Breton, which was newer. See Mine A Breton. P.O. 1827-1861, 1863-1969.

Old Monroe (Lincoln). The original county seat, the name was Monroe. It was changed to avoid confusion with Monroe City in Monroe County (RF). P.O. 1863-now. Pop. 242.

Olympia (Cedar). This name was selected by the postal service from a list submitted by the first postmaster. It was popular at the time, and in use in other states (RF). P.O. 1899-1907.

Omaha
Osage Beach

Omaha [OH muh haw] (Putnam). Originally named Cross Roads (RF), the new name is taken from the Osage word *umaha*, meaning "upstream people" (JL).

One Hundred and Two River. Two possibilities: This river is 102 miles in length; military surveyors determined it is 102 miles from Fort Leavenworth (RF).

Onondaga Cave State Park. Owners considered several Native American names for this cave. *Onondaga*, which is supposed to mean "people of the hills," comes from a tribe who lived in New York.

Oran [oh RAN] (Scott). Named for a North African port city, this settlement was first called Sylvania, a name in use in Dade County, then St. Cloud. P.O. 1870-now. Pop. 1,164.

Oregon [AW ri guhn] or [AH ri guhn] (Holt). In 1841, when this city was laid out, Oregon territory was just opened up, so the name is in honor of that new territory (VR). See Oregon County. P.O. 1843-now. Pop. 935.

Oregon County. This name is a result of "Oregon Fever" that swept Missouri in the 1840s. With Missouri Senator Lewis Fields Linn at the front, the United States and Britain battled over the possession of Oregon Territory. A year after the county was organized, the issue was settled in favor of the United States. The name, of Native American origin, comes from the Oregon River, now called the Columbia River (RF). See also Linn County, Oregon Trail. Organized 1845. Pop. 9,427.

Oregon Trail, The. In the late 1830s and until his death in 1843, Missouri Senator Lewis Fields Linn worked to open Oregon for American settlement. A few years after he died, a steady flow of people migrated west on the trail, which wound 2,000 miles over plains, across rivers and through the mountains (DM). See also Linn County, Oregon County.

Osage Beach [OH sayj] or [oh SAYJ] (Camden). This town developed in the late 1930s upon completion of the Bagnell Dam hydroelectric project and the Lake of the Ozarks. Taking its name from the Osage River, it is situated along the ridge above the lake (RF). See Osage River. P.O. 1935-now. Pop. 2,599.

Osage City (Cole). This town is located at the junction of the Osage with the Missouri, and is named for the river. See Osage River. P.O. 1856-1962.

Osage County. This county is named for the river which forms its western boundary. See Osage River. Pop 12,018.

Osage River. An important tributary of the Missouri River, this is named for the people living there when the French arrived. The Osage were described by Lewis and Clark as strong and peaceful, "the largest and best-formed Indians" who had "made advance in agriculture." Sometimes you'll see the name written Washashe, and you'll hear that *Washashe* means "war people" (JL) or "the strong" (DE). For a long time, explorers struggled with the name, spelling it Washashe, Huzzah, Hoozaw, Wasbasha, Ozages, Oua-chage, and Ausage. Finally, the spelling was standardized, but old spellings survive as place names.

Osceola [OH see oh luh] (St. Clair) county seat. This name replaced Crossing of the Osage at Crow and Crutchfield. Osceola was the name of a well-known Seminole chief (RF). P.O. 1839-now. Pop. 755.

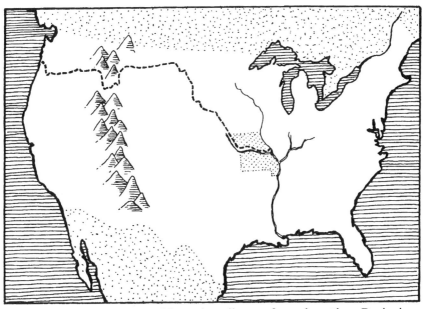

The Oregon Trail was one of the main trails west for early settlers. Beginning in the 1840s, a steady flow of people migrated west on the trail, which wound 2,000 miles over plains, across rivers and through the mountains

Osiris
Ozark Mountains

Osiris [oh SEYE ris] (Cedar). This is the name of the Egyptian god of light, health and agriculture. It was chosen by the postmaster, who was looking for a name that was different (RF).

Oskaloosa [ah skuh LOO suh] (Barton). This town was named for the hometown of the settlers: Oskaloosa, Iowa (RF). P.O. 1894-1953.

Oto (Stone). This town was named for the Otoe Native Americans, but the thrifty post office preferred to leave off the final "e" to save ink (LI). P.O. 1877-1913.

Ottery Creek (Iron). Even though there are seven creeks named Otter Creek, and lakes, ponds and schools named for the playful critter, this creek was named for a local landowner, John Autrey.

Owensville (Gasconade). A blacksmith named Luster and a storekeeper named Owen were the first two businessmen at this site. To determine which name the town should bear, the two agreed to settle with a game of horseshoes. Luster won, but consoled the loser by letting him name the town. "Owensville sounds better than Lusterville," said the good-hearted blacksmith (LI). Another version has Owens winning fair and square (RF). P.O. 1856-now. Pop. 2,325.

Owl Creek. There are at least ten creeks bearing this name, attesting to the numbers of owls that once lived in the state.

Ozark [OH zahrk] (Christian) county seat. This town is named for the mountains. P.O. 1840-now. Pop. 4,243.

Ozark County. Organized in 1841, the county was named for the mountains. Most of the early residents came from Georgia, and residents requested that the county name be changed from Ozark to Decatur, for Decatur, Georgia. It was so changed by the legislature in 1843. It was changed back by the next administration in 1845 (RF). Pop. 8,598.

Ozark Mountains [OH zahrks]. This is a very old mountain range in south Missouri. Early French explorers liked to abbreviate the names of Native American tribes, so they wrote on their maps "Aux Arcs," meaning that the wooded hills were home to the Arkansas Indians. Pronounced, this sounded like Ozark. Also called Ozark Highland and "the Ozarks."

P

Pacific (Franklin). Originally named Franklin, this town was planned as a stop on the Atlantic and Pacific Railroad, which was to connect St. Louis with both coasts. Work on the line halted in 1853 when the builders ran out of money. At about the same time, the town applied for a post office and learned there was another Franklin in Missouri. The town name was changed to Pacific, in honor of the railroad's hoped-for destination. Now the railroad could claim that it reached Pacific, and the line's name was changed to Missouri Pacific Railroad or MOPAC (RF). P.O. 1854-now. Pop. 4,358.

Paddy Creek (Texas). First called Paddy's Rock, in pioneer days this Piney River place was dangerous for log rafters. One named Paddy sank a lumber raft here, and drowned. It is about 3.25 miles north of Hazelton (GA).

"Paincourt" or "Short of Bread" (St. Louis City). This is an early nickname for St. Louis, indicating either that it was poor, or that the bakers shorted customers with their product.

Paint Brush Prairie (Pettis). This public land is named for the bright red Indian paintbrush plant which was in bloom the first time the Department of Conservation naming committee visited.

Painted Rock and Paint Rock. Two state forests, are the sites of Native American pictographs.

Paitzdorf (Perry). Now called Unionville, this is one of five towns in Perry County founded by a group of German Lutheran immigrants in the first wave of migration. Paitzdorf, Germany, was the home parish of one of the pastors (RF). See Altenburg.

Palace (Pulaski). In a reverse of the usual trend, this town was named for a school, which was probably named for a family. The town had nearly withered away when a CCC camp was established there, giving it a second life (RF). P.O. 1909, 1931-1957. There was also a Palace in Greene County (P.O. 1888-1905).

Palmyra [pal MEYE ruh] (Marion) county seat. The first name proposed for this settlement was Springfield because it is surrounded by seven never-failing springs that feed a stream running through the old part of town (RF). However, the town was given a Biblical name, that of the Syrian city built by King Solomon (VR). Nicknamed the "City of Flowers" and the "Athens of Missouri," Palmyra had three colleges and two academies in the mid-1800s (RF). Mark Twain nicknamed it "Constantinople," and called nearby Marion City "Napoleon." P.O. 1820-now. Pop. 3,371.

Panther (Oregon). Missourians can point to at least 25 place names referring to the big cat, now extinct here (GS). P.O. 1883-1884.

Paradise (Clay). First named Gosneyville for a local blacksmith, the village never had an official layout (APM). The name was changed and the town established when settlers came fleeing religious persecution (RF). P.O. 1858-1863, 1865-1907.

Paris [PAIR is] (Monroe) county seat. This is one of the county seats in the region known as Little Dixie, and rooted in southern heritage. "The Friendliest Town North of Dixie" was named for, and is modeled after Paris, Kentucky. Early residents from Kentucky and Tennessee immediately built the essentials for comfortable living—a courthouse, a tavern and a race track west of town (VR). P.O. 1841-now. Pop. 1,486.

Park Hills (St. Francois). In 1994, the towns of Elvins, Esther, Flat River and Rivermines gave up their identities to form one new town. By combining administration and services, they hope to become more efficient and competitive in attracting new businesses. The new name was chosen from 1,000 submissions. It suggests the location, between several state parks, and the hilly terrain (LI).

Parkville (Platte). Named for Colonel George S. Park, the town at the junction of the Missouri and Platte Rivers boasted storehouses, shops and a large hotel. Park's buildings were donated to the Presbyterian Church for Park College (CG). Pop. 2,402.

Parnell (Nodaway). This town was named for the Irish statesman Charles Stewart Parnell, by a freedom-loving settler (RF). P.O. 1887-now. Pop. 157.

Passaic [puh SAY ik] (Bates). A rarity in Missouri, this town was named for an eastern (New Jersey) city (RF). P.O. 1889-now. Pop. 40.

Patty's Cave (Butler). This is a cavern near Cane Creek where southern sympathizers hid military provisions from guerilla raiders from the north (RF).

Paw Paw. Towns in Buchanan, New Madrid and Sullivan Counties and a valley in Webster County used this name. Pawpaw fruit, nicknamed "Missouri banana," tastes like a "well-prepared custard."

Peace Valley (Howell). This name was given for early residents. One of them was known as Grandaddy Peace in the region (RF). P.O. 1876-now.

Peach Orchard (Pemiscot). An early settler planted peaches here, but was flooded out. Years later, when the area was drained and a settlement planned, remainders of the orchard were discovered (RF). P.O. 1936-1973.

Peculiar [pi KYOOL yuhr] (Cass). This town was named when a group of spiritualists came to examine the property they hoped to homestead. One of them declared, "That's peculiar! It is the very place I saw in a vision in Connecticut" (VR). Another story swears that the town was named by a tired postmaster who had sent many post office applications to Washington, only to have them all rejected. He was told to try something new or "peculiar," and he did (RF). P.O. 1868-now. Pop. 1,777.

Peers (Warren). Peers was named after Judge Charles E. Peers, an attorney for the railroad and founder of the *Warrenton Banner* newspaper (LI).

Pekitanoui. This Native American word was used by Father Marquette in his journals. The word *Pekitanoui*, which means Muddy River, or River of the Big Canoes, is seldom used, but the river is still sometimes called by its nickname, "Big Muddy."

Pelican Island
Perry

Pelican Island. Over the years, numbers of these huge birds have been seen resting here on their migratory flight (CG).

Pemiscot County [PEM i skaht]. The county is named for Pemiscot River. See Pemiscot River. Pop. 21,921.

Pemiscot River. A Native American name that may mean "liquid mud," or "runs next to" (RF). Either meaning fits the muddy swamp that settlers found next to the Mississippi River in southeast Missouri. Sometimes you'll hear "Pemiscot Bayou." *Bayou* translates to "river," a linguistic memento of the original French settlers (LI). One old French pronunciation of Pemiscot made the "o" long as in "soda" and the "t" silent. That pronunciation is rarely heard nowadays.

Penitentiary Bend (McDonald). A cave on this bend of Big Sugar Creek was the headquarters of a gang of bandits. There is a high bluff on one side and the creek on the other, so they felt their hideout could only be approached by boat. The bad guys were caught when clever law men rigged up a bridge just out of their line of vision (LI).

Pennytown (Saline). This town was founded after the Civil War by Joseph Penny, a free African American from Kansas. He came to Missouri to farm, and saved enough money to buy eight acres. A blacksmith came to set up shop, and a school and a church were built. By 1880, 200 African American people lived in Pennytown. Today, the church still stands, but the town is gone (LI).

Perche Creek. The sources give us several choices: (1) The name is a French word meaning "furrow" or "ditch"; (2) an Osage word, *paci*, meaning "hilltop" (CG); (3) because the creek has high limestone bluffs on both sides, Perche comes from *roche perche*, meaning "split rock" (RF); (4) the creek is full of perch fish (LI).

Perchetown (Boone). Named for the creek and first called "town of Persia," promoters offered free lots to merchants and mechanics (CG). It was briefly headquarters for a mail contractor, with his carriage and repair shops, stables and granaries. All were washed away by the creek (APM).

Perry [PER ee] (Ralls). One of the gateway towns to Mark Twain Lake, the town was named for its first postmaster, William Perry Crosthwaite (RF). P.O. 1866-now. Pop. 711.

Perry County [PER ee]. The county with the most caves in the state, it was named for Captain Oliver Hazard Perry, a great naval hero of the War of 1812. Perry won the battle of Lake Erie on September 19, 1813, and sent General Harrison the famous message: "We have met the enemy and they are ours." Organized 1820. Pop. 16,648.

Perryville (Perry) county seat. The name of the town was derived from that of the county. See Perry County. P.O. 1823-now. Pop. 6,933.

Pershing (Gasconade). First called Potsdam by German settlers, this town was renamed during World War I due to anti-German feelings. The new name honors General John J. Pershing, national hero and Missouri native. See Pershing State Park. P.O. Potsdam 1894-1918, Pershing 1918-1959.

Pershing State Park (Linn and Livingston). Dedicated to the memory of General John J. Pershing, World War I commander of the American Expeditionary Forces in Europe. The large frame Victorian house where Pershing lived in Laclede is a State Historic Site and is open for public tours (LI).

Peruque [puh ROOK] (St. Charles). Named for Peruque Creek, the original settlement here was called La Perruque, probably a family name. Later, a bustling river town, called Beck's Landing, became site of a railroad bridge across Dardenne Creek. During the Civil War, the Union Army built a fort, Fort Peruque, to protect the bridge (LI). P.O. 1888-1979.

Pettis County [PET is]. U.S. Representative Spencer Darwin Pettis (1802-1831) was born in Virginia and came to Howard County as a young man. An influential Democrat, his political career was cut short after his successful campaign for a second term in Congress. In the heated campaign, he supported Andrew Jackson, therefore opposed the National Bank. He was challenged to a duel by Thomas Biddle, who managed the National Bank in Missouri, and they were both mortally wounded. Pettis died the next day (DM). Organized 1833. Pop. 35,437.

Pevely [PEEV lee] (Jefferson). There are dozens of unsolved name mysteries, and this is one. P.O. 1858-now. Pop. 2,831.

Phelps County [FELPS]. Named for John Phelps (1814-1886), a Democrat and popular congressman at that time, who in 1877 became governor of Missouri (RF). A native of Connecticut, Phelps was a Union officer during the Civil War. Organized 1837. Pop. 35,248.

Philadelphia (Marion). This town was named for Philadelphia, Pennsylvania, birthplace of the United States of America. P.O. 1847-now.

Pickle Springs Natural Area (Ste. Francois). Named for a family, this Missouri Department of Conservation area has a two-mile trail through hoodoos, or sandstone rock pillars, and deep canyons. Ice, wind and rain have eroded the sandstone outcropping into unusual shapes (LI).

Pierpont (Boone). When an 1834 fire destroyed Boone County's first recorded distillery and grist mill, the building was used to house Missouri's first paper mill. The distillery proved to be more profitable, however, and the mill soon reverted to its original pursuit (LI). The building was originally located where Rock Bridge State Park now sits. In 1889, the store and blacksmith shop were moved to the top of the hill. The new site was named Pierpont, a French-sounding name conjured up by Americans and meaning "rock bridge." The Pierpont Store is located 85 feet directly above the Pierpont Dome of the Devil's Icebox Cave, located in Rock Bridge State Park, 1.5 miles away (PW).

Pike County [PEYEK]. Founded just after the steamboat *Zebulon Pike* began traveling the Mississippi, this county was named for Brigadier General Zebulon Montgomery Pike. The popular explorer was discoverer of Pike's Peak. The term *Piker* originated in San Francisco, after 200 men from Pike County migrated to California during the Gold Rush. Knickerbocker Magazine of 1857 explained that Pikers "applied to Missourians from Pike County, but afterwards used to designate individuals presenting a happy compound of verdancy and ruffianism" (VR). Pop. 15,969.

Pike's Defeat (Texas). This treacherous bend on the Big Piney River was named for Bill Pike, an early log rafter who sunk his load here; it is ten miles north of Hazelton (GA).

Pilot Grove (Cooper). An ancient grove of hickory trees on the high prairie was a landmark (or "pilot") for people traveling from Boonville and Franklin to the southwest (RF). The Katy Railroad reached Pilot Grove on May 18, 1873. Within a decade, there were four general stores, one drugstore, a hardware store, two tin shops, a furniture store, a saddle and harness shop, three blacksmith and wagon shops, a restaurant, a lumberyard, two hotels, a barber shop and a shoemaker (LI). P.O. 1833-now. Pop. 714.

Pilot Knob (Iron). There are hills called Pilot Knob in Iron, Madison, Phelps, Stone and Taney Counties, named because of their shapes and visibility as landmarks or "pilots." This Iron County hill is rich in iron, and a mining town there and took the name (RF). P.O. 1858-now. Pop. 793.

Pilot Knob (Madison). About 600 feet high, this was the site of an important battle won by the Federal side during the Civil War; it was known to the Confederate side as Oak Hill (LI). P.O. 1851, 1854-1858. Pop. 767.

Pin Oak (Gasconade). This round, still body of water on the Gasconade was overhung with pin oaks and water oaks (CG).

Pine Run. "Run" is a synonym for "creek" in the local dialect around Galena, but this was unknown to the highway department. Their sign says "Pine Run Creek" (LI).

Pineville (McDonald) county seat. Some say this town was named for the pine forest nearby. Some say it was named for Pineville, Kentucky (RF). In German tradition, visiting pine forests was supposed to be good for your health due to the "ozone" therein (LI). P.O. 1849-1864, 1866-now. Pop. 580.

Piney Creek. The Ozarker loved to use the "ey" ending, which changes a noun to an adjective. We find creeks named Deerey, Piney, Brushy, Clifty, Gravelly, and Caney, all in southwest Missouri.

Piney River Narrows Wildlife Area (Texas). Log rafters had a spot they called Narrow Gap near here. Log rafts had to negotiate between stumps on both banks (GA).

Pioneer (Barry). This town was named "in honor of all early settlers" (RF). P.O. 1883-1934.

Pittsburg (Hickory). This town was named for a Pitts family, early settlers, who probably chose "burg" rather than "ville" or "town" to suggest the city in Pennsylvania. The familiar name has been adopted by 14 American towns (RF). P.O. 1846-now.

Plad [PLAD] (Dallas). The post office misprinted the town name, Glad, and it was too hard to get the mistake corrected. People decided to go ahead and call the town Plad (LI). P.O. 1891-1960. Pop. 30.

Plato
Platte River

Plato [PLAY toh] (Dallas). Our Missouri grandfathers delighted in their classical educations, so it was natural that one town at least would be named for the legendary philosopher and writer of ancient Athens. This town was planned as an ideal community, like that described by Plato in <u>The Republic</u>. P.O. 1891-1960.

Platte City [PLAT] (Platte) county seat. This town was first known as Falls of Platte, or Platte Falls, from the falls in the stream. Later for a time it was known as Martinsville for Zadoc Martin, who operated a ferry on the river. See Platte River. P.O. 1839-now. Pop. 2,947.

Platte County. The county is named for its principal waterway, the Platte River (RF). See Platte River. Organized 1838. Pop. 57,867.

Platte River. This major tributary of the Missouri River in northwest Missouri was called Petite Riviere Platte by the French and the Little Platte River by Lewis and Clark. The translation is "little shallow river" (VR). *Platte* is French for "flat" or "shallow." There was a town named for the river. P.O. 1848-1861, 1863-1905.

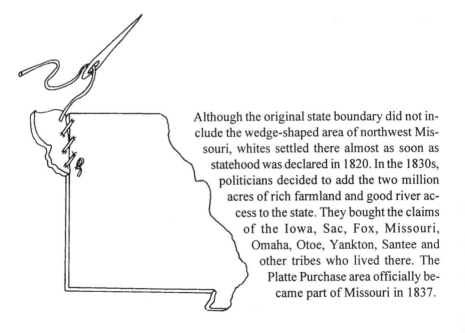

Although the original state boundary did not include the wedge-shaped area of northwest Missouri, whites settled there almost as soon as statehood was declared in 1820. In the 1830s, politicians decided to add the two million acres of rich farmland and good river access to the state. They bought the claims of the Iowa, Sac, Fox, Missouri, Omaha, Otoe, Yankton, Santee and other tribes who lived there. The Platte Purchase area officially became part of Missouri in 1837.

Plattsburg (Clinton). First named Concord, then Springfield, unlucky residents learned both names were in use other places in Missouri. The present name came from a town in Clinton County, New York (APM). During the first winter, the town's first resident said he killed 48 black bears here, 22 of them in one elm tree. The present-day courthouse, now bearless, is on the site of that tree. Here also is the monument to David Rice Atchison (see Atchison County) (VR). P.O. 1835-now. Pop. 2,248.

Pleasant Green (Cooper). This town was an important shipping point in the 1800s. It was named for a major landowner, Presley Green (RF). P.O. 1842-1867, 1869-1871.

Pleasant Hill. This name has been used by at least three towns and dozens of churches and schools in the state, most so-named because of their delightful locations. Pop. 3,827.

Pleasant Hope (Polk). First called Lick Skillet, perhaps for its greed and poverty. There, a "little academy" was founded by Cumberland Presbyterians who had a pleasant hope for it (RF). P.O. 1851-now. Pop. 360.

Plevna [PLEV nuh] (Knox). First called Owl Creek, the name was changed to the nickname of John Naylor, the town founder. His nickname may have been inspired by news that, after 143 days of fighting, the Russians had defeated the Turks in Pleven, North Bulgaria (RF). In 1877, the story of this Bulgarian city under siege from Russians was well known to freedom-loving Americans (GS). P.O. 1877-now.

Pocahantas [poh kuh HAHN tuhs] (Cape Girardeau). This name may have been given to tease the largest landowner in the region, who claimed he was descended from the Native American princess. P.O. 1856-now. Pop. 90.

Polar Bear Cave (McDonald). In the 1930s when this show cave opened to the public, the local name Polar Cave given for its cold temperature, was changed to attract attention (RF).

Pole Branch (Johnson). This tributary of Black Jack Creek was named for the little trees which grew thickly on its banks.

Pole Cats Branch (Clay). Pole cat is another name for skunk. Besides this branch or creek, there is a Pole Cat Creek in Harrison County named by honey hunters, the first white men to explore the country (RF).

Polk County
Poosey

Polk County [POHK]. John P. Campbell, a prominent citizen who was second cousin to Congressman James K. Polk, later President Polk, suggested they name the county Polk (RF). Organized 1835. Pop. 21,826.

Polo (Caldwell). This town was named for a farming community in Illinois (RF). P.O. 1868-now. Pop. 539.

Pomme de Terre [PUHM duh tahr] or [PUHM duh tayr]. The river, man-made lake and the public lands all take their name from the discovery by the French of potato-like plants growing on the original river's banks (RF). Potatoes were new to the French; they are new-world plants and there was no French name before its discovery. *Pomme de terre* can be translated into English "apple of the earth" (LI). This place name may go back as far as 1682 when, local legend claims, Robert de la Salle visited the area (RF). The name was Americanized in 1795, when a mapmaker noted Great Potato River, and Meriwether Clark dubbed it Wild Potatoe Creek, but the American names didn't stick. P.O. 1840-1842.

Pomona (Howell, St. Charles, Knox). She is the Roman goddess of fruit trees, often invoked to name fruit-growing regions (GS). P.O. (St. Charles) 1851-1854, (Howell) 1895-now.

Ponce de Leon [PAWN si duh LEE uhn] (Stone). Locally called Ponce [PAWN see], this historic health resort was named for the famous 17th-century Spanish explorer who spent his life looking for the fountain of youth (RF). P.O. 1881-now.

Pontiac (Ozark). This was named for the town in Michigan (RF). The chief and warrior (ca. 1720-1765) battled the English but made peace in his last years; he was much admired by early settlers for his character (GS). P.O. 1887-now.

Poor Man Diggings (Franklin). This shallow lead-mining area could be worked with a pick and shovel (RF).

Poosey (Livingston and Grundy). This region was named for a part of Kentucky that was the home of a similarly named tribe of Native Americans. Outsiders have generally thought that Poosey County or Poosey Country was a local name for a "mythical country . . . which cannot be exactly located" (VR). Residents, however, insist the community was real. Schools, stores and churches were isolated by the rough, hilly terrain. Good roads and electricity missed the place. Today, the name is preserved by Poosey State Forest, managed by the Department of Conservation (LI).

Poplar Bluff [PAHP luhr BLUHF] (Butler) county seat. Originally a government town, 160 acres were selected by county commissioners for a county seat. Its name was suggested by the famous tulip tree, commonly called poplar, the magnolia of the North, which at that time covered the bluffs overlooking the river (RF). P.O. 1850-now. Pop. 16,996.

Port Scipio (Marion). Named for a rival of the famous General Hannibal, in history Scipio contributed to Hannibal's defeat. In Missouri, Hannibal won (RF). Today, Port Scipio is the site of a boat club on the Mississippi River (LI). See Hannibal.

Portage des Sioux [por TAYJ day SOO] or [por TAYJ di soo] (St. Charles). According to an 1837 record, this site was named when the Sioux and Missouris were at war in the area. The Missouri planned an ambush at the mouth of the Missouri River, but the Sioux, instead of descending as expected, landed at the portage and crossed overland with their canoes on their backs (VR). P.O. 1819-1827, 1833-1847, 1857-1867, 1871-now. Pop. 503.

Portageville [POHR tuhj vil] (New Madrid). Part of the boundary line between Pemiscot and New Madrid Counties was formed by an early portage line between the St. Francois and Mississippi Rivers. This town is close to that line (RF). P.O. 1873-now. Pop. 3,401.

Portland (Callaway). A natural port on the Missouri River, this was an active river shipping town, established in 1831, where railroad ties, tobacco, barrels of hops, and livestock were all boarded for St. Louis. Portland was the only Callaway County town of importance along the river before the railroad came, but once the route was established, the railroad towns of Wainwright, Tebbetts, Mokane and Steedman quickly appeared (BD). Count Adelbert Baudissin, thinking it was an "up and coming" town in the Missouri River Valley, settled near Portland in the 1850s. In an account he states, " . . . the thing for me to do is to direct German emigrants to Portland because I have the firm conviction that business people as well as landowners would find their good fortune at this place." At the time the population of Portland was around 200, and eight or ten riverboats docked at the town each week. The town continued to thrive when the railroad came through. According to a local resident, the town's depot was quite nice with a large waiting room. But it was later torn down, and replaced by a "little two by four thing" (BD). P.O. 1832-now (BH). Pop. 160.

Possum Trot (Pemiscot). Many Missouri places are named for the opossum. This name suggests that the openings between trees were so narrow only a 'possum could trot through them (RF).

Potosi [puh TOH see] or [puh TOH suh] (Washington) county seat. Built by Moses Austin, this name is a short version of the name of a famous silver-mining district in Mexico, San Luis Potosi (RF). Sometimes, you'll hear local people putting on a fancier pronunciation: [POH tuh SEE]. P.O. 1824-now. Pop. 2,683.

Potsdam (Gasconade). See Pershing.

Prairie du Chien (Harrison). This prairie was home to many prairie dogs. *Chien* means "dog" in French. (LI).

Prairie State Park (Barton). This remnant of prairie, with its resident buffalo herd, is named for the expanse that covered half of our state (LI).

Prathersville (Clay). This town was named for the mill owner. P.O. 1876-1904. Pop. 130.

Princeton (Mercer) county seat. After naming the county Mercer, citizens named the seat of government for the Battle of Princeton, fought in 1777, at which Americans led by General Hugh Mercer defeated the British (VR). Princeton was the birthplace of Martha Jane Canary, Calamity Jane, who rode with the Pony Express and scouted for General Custer. P.O. 1846-now. Pop. 1,021.

Prohibition (Montgomery). This post office was managed by an auction-eer-mail carrier who was against the use of alcohol (LI). P.O. 1890-1914.

Prohibition City (Worth). First named Smithton, the town was renamed to note the fact that the founder was a temperance supporter (RF). P.O. 1877-1881.

Protem [proh TEM] (Taney). This name, from the Latin *pro tempore*, means "temporary." It was supposed to be a stopgap name to give arguing citizens time to settle on a permanent one (LI). P.O. 1875-now.

Providence (Boone). This old river site was named by a band of settlers from Tennessee who saw their original town, Nashville, swept away by the Missouri River flood of 1844. They moved farther up the bluff, taking the name Providence to symbolize both their acceptance of the loss and hope for the future (RF). Nashville was named for resident Ira Nash, known as either (1) "the most quarrelsome man in Missouri" (CG) or (2) "an eccentric genius" (RF). P.O. 1844-1846, 1853-1854, 1857-1918.

Pucky Huddle. See Davisville.

Pulaski County [puh LAS kee] or [puh LAS keye]. Named for Count Casimir Pulaski, the Polish revolutionary, who fought for the American colonies in the Revolutionary War and was killed at the battle of Savannah (RF). Pulaski was dubbed "the father of American cavalry," and fought with General Wayne. (The county seat is Waynesville.) Organized 1833. Pop. 41,307.

Pulaskifield (Barry). This community was founded by Polish immigrants in 1892, named for the Polish revolutionary. See Pulaski County.

Pulltight (Shannon). At the bottom of a steep hill was a grist mill. Descending the hill with a loaded wagon, the driver had to pull tight on the reins. P.O. 1889-1907.

Punkin Center (Howell). The name was suggested by a comic phonograph record (RF), and natives still call it and spell it Punkin Center (LI). The Missouri Highway Department won the spelling bee, and changed the word on highway signs to "Pumpkin."

Purdin (Linn). This settlement was named for the landowner who deeded 37 acres to the railroad for a town. P.O. 1877-now. Pop. 217.

Putnam County [PUHT nuhm]. Named for General Israel Putnam, a Revolutionary War hero, the county was part of the dispute between Iowa and Missouri over a strip of territory 9 miles wide which was claimed by both states. In 1851 the U.S. Supreme Court awarded the land to Iowa (RF). Organized 1845. Pop. 5,079.

Puxico [PUHK si koh] (Stoddard). This town is named for the Shawnee chief who camped in this region before settlement times (Enc). P.O. 1884-now. Pop. 819.

Q

Quarantine (St. Louis). This special town on the Mississippi River near St. Louis was founded for people with contagious diseases. P.O. 1893-1910.

Queen City (Schuyler). Laid out by developers as "Queen of the Prairie," this town prospered with the fortunes of the railroad. General stores, hotels, shippers and blacksmith shops were quickly joined by drug stores, dressmakers and photographer studios (LI). P.O. 1866-now. Pop. 704.

Quercus (Butler). Charles Langlots named Quercus, Latin for "oak." This railroad switch was the loading point for the Quercus Lumber Company of East Poplar Bluff. The oak was king of Missouri's native trees. G.C. Swallow, state geologist and professor at University of Missouri-Columbia, wrote in 1856 about finding a Spanish Oak (*Quercus falcota*) measuring 28 feet in circumference and 100 feet in height (RF). Latin tree names given to other Butler County lumber towns were: Celtis, Fagus, Ilex, Nyssa, Platanus and Ulmus.

R

Racket (Benton). The original owners of the small general store were always fighting. One day a neighbor, dreading the trip to the post office, said "Well, guess I'll go to racket to get the mail," and the term stuck (LI). P.O. 1897-1936.

Radical (Stone). This town was site of the Kimberling Ferry across the White River. Now buried under Table Rock Lake, it was named for residents who were Radical Republicans (LI).

Ralls County [RAWLZ]. This county was named for State Representative Daniel Ralls, a Virginian who emigrated in his youth to Kentucky, then to Missouri. In 1820, when the general assembly was electing Missouri's first U.S. senators, Ralls was in bed and dying. He asked to be carried in for the vote and could barely say the names, "Barton and Benton." His colleagues were, indeed, elected (RF). Organized 1820. Pop. 8,476.

Randolph County [RAN dahlf]. John Randolph of Roanoke, Virginia, was an orator and statesman of renown. He was born in Chesterfield, Virginia, June 2, 1773, educated at Princeton and Columbia Universities, and died in Philadelphia on June 24, 1833. He served Virginia as member of the U.S. House of Representatives for several terms and as a U.S. senator (RF). Organized 1829. Pop. 24,370.

Rat (Shannon). The postmaster's revenge: He first requested for his office the name Buckshorn because he had a nice rack of horns hanging over the door, but the department rejected it (RF). A second story goes that the postmaster requested names of each of his three daughters. Each name was already in use. The frustrated fellow was complaining about this to a customer when a rat ran out from a sack of seed corn. The customer said Rat would make a good name. The postmaster submitted it and the name was cleared for use (GC). P.O. 1898-1954.

Rural Free Delivery Mail

Missouri grew fast after Lewis and Clark came back from their famous 1804-1806 exploration of the Missouri River. Entrepreneurs came here, looking for furs, minerals, timber and other natural resources that could be mined or harvested for urban populations in the East. Farmers came here, looking for nutrient-rich, cheap land on which to stake a claim. Business people came here, ready to set up shop to service the new population.

To the isolated pioneer, the arrival of precious words and news from far-off family members was treasured for months. In early Missouri, letters and packages were carried by private carriers—via steamship companies, by overland stagecoach and, briefly, from St. Joseph to California by the Pony Express.

Postal service by the U.S. government was an improvement over irregular delivery by private carriers, but was slow to develop. Rural neighborhoods, isolated by poor roads, had an especially hard time obtaining mail service. General stores applied to become post office representatives. When application was made, local names were often thought unflattering and were changed. The name of Pucky Huddle (Crawford County) was changed to the more refined Davisville. Toad Suck (Cape Girardeau County) became Millersville. Exist (Wayne County), a name appropriate for a place where people could barely get by, was changed to Burch.

In 1886, the post office ordered that names had to be different from each other. Of the many Cross Roads and Stringtowns, well known to the local populations, there could only officially be one of each. Cross Roads in Iron, St. Clair and Dade Counties became Belleview, Damascus and Everton. Also in 1886, prefixes like "East" and suffixes like "-boro," and "-burgh" were forbidden in new town names. In 1894, the post office went a step further and ordered "from this date only short names or names of one word will be accepted . . ."

Post office requirements gave people a new way to complain about the government and as a result we have some of our best place name stories. Some of the stories were no doubt made up after the names were adopted. The requirement that names be distinct is part of the explanations for Peculiar, Rat, and Ink. The requirement that names be short was taken to mean three letters; the result was town names just three letters long—from Abo to Zig.

Ray County [RAY]. This county was named for John Ray, a delegate to the Constitutional Convention of 1820; he died during that convention. The county was nicknamed "The Free State of Ray" because it originally covered such a large territory—all of Missouri north of the Missouri River and west of the Grand (VR). Organized 1820. Pop. 21,971.

Raytown (Jackson). This village, first called Ray, was probably named for an early settler (RF). P.O. 1871-1902, 1915-1956. Pop. 30,601.

Readsville (Callaway). This town was settled by John A. Read, who was the first postmaster (RF). P.O. 1856-1861, 1863-1954.

Rebel's Cove (Schuyler). This Department of Conservation property was nearly named Parson's Bend, Snake Den or Coal Holler. Since the property had been owned by Henry Clay Dean, an orator who won fame by standing up for the southern cause, the family petitioned for the name to remain the one he gave it (LI).

Reform (Callaway). Local folks, who loved to tell that they went to Reform School, thought the tiny town may have been named for a religious group that only stayed a short time (LI). The small farming community was demolished by the construction of the Callaway Nuclear Plant in the 1970s. P.O. 1853-1907.

Rensselaer [RENS uhl uhr] or [ren suh LEER] (Ralls). The town was named for a Presbyterian prep school associated with the Rensselaer Institute in Troy, New York. The school was also known as "Van Rensselaer Academy" for the founder (RF). P.O. 1871-1953.

Republic (Greene). The name was given by the founder, a patriotic man. P.O. 1871-now. Pop. 6,292.

Rex City (Jasper). *Rex*, Latin for king, was supplied by founders who expected the town would be significant. The place name, Rex, was also used by post offices in Morgan (1898) and Polk (1900-1906) Counties. P.O. 1893-1895.

Reynolds County [REN lds] or [REN lz]. This county is named for Governor Thomas Reynolds (1796-1844) of Howard County, who is noted for writing the shortest act in the history of the Missouri legislature. It was:

"Imprisonment for debt is hereby abolished." His death occurred just a year before the county was organized (RF). Organized 1845. Pop. 6,661.

Rhineland (Montgomery). This town was settled by Germans as early as 1837. The location was moved in 1892 when the MKT Railroad was laid out next to the river, but the railroad retained the name (RF). After the flood of 1993, some of the homes were moved to higher ground. See Missouri Rhineland. P.O. 1853-now. Pop. 157.

Rich Fountain (Osage). This town was named by Father Ferdinand Benoit Marie Guislain Helias d'Huddeghem, or Father Helias, for the many clear springs in the area (VR). P.O. 1854-1972.

Rich Hill (Bates). Two versions: It was named by the first postmaster for the town's location by a hill that was rich with coal (VR); it was named by a corporation of businessmen, Rich Hill Town Company (APM). P.O. 1871-now. Pop. 1,317.

Richland (Pulaski). This name has been given to three towns, and dozens of creeks, schools and churches. In most cases, it alludes to the richness of the soil. P.O. (New Madrid) 1820-1827, (Greene) 1840-1867, (Pulaski) 1869-now. Pop. 2,029.

Richmond (Ray) county seat. Named by settlers from Virginia in honor of the capital of their state (RF). Bloody Bill Anderson, the pro-southern guerrilla leader, is buried here. P.O. 1828-now. Pop. 5,738.

Ripley County [RIP lee]. This county is named for General Eleanor W. Ripley (1782-1839) of the War of 1812, who was famed for the defense of Fort Erie on August 15, 1814. General Ripley was a member of Congress from Louisiana from 1835 to 1839 (RF). Organized 1833. Pop. 12,303.

Rivermines (St. Francois). First called Central because of the Central Lead Company, the name was changed when Doe Run Lead Company took over. The town merged with others to become Park Hills in 1994. See Park Hills.

Rives County [REEVZ]. Part of this short-lived county went to Henry County and part to Saint Clair. The name honored William Rives, who served in the Revolutionary War and was elected to the Senate in later years. When Rives joined the Whig party, Democrats in the county agitated to change the name.

Roach
Rockaway Beach

Roach (Camden). Not named for the bug, this town bears the name of prominent early settlers. P.O. 1886-1897, 1903-now.

Roanoke [ROH uh nohk] (Randolph). This town was named for Roanoke, Virginia, birthplace of John Randolph (RF). See Randolph County. P.O. 1838-1871.

Roaring River (Barry). This is a descriptive name, given because the water roars out of the cave at its source (RF). P.O. 1854-1864, 1871-1894.

Rocheport [ROHSH port] (Boone). Citizens wanted to name this town Rock Port, but a French missionary prevailed upon them to keep the traditional French. Despite its rocky landing, the town was an important shipping point for flatboats, keelboats and steamboats (CG). Located on the Missouri River at the mouth of the Moniteau Creek, Rocheport grew rapidly as steamboat traffic increased. In 1849, 57 steamboats made 500 landings at Rocheport (BD). This river town was called "our capital" by Bloody Bill Anderson and his bushwhackers (VR). The Missouri Kansas and Texas Railroad tunnel, 240 foot long, was built in 1893. During construction of the line, the tunnel was held hostage for several weeks when laborers for the McCormick Company seized the tunnel and demanded higher wages. The workers threatened to blow up the bluff if work on the line resumed. After three weeks, sheriffs of Howard and Boone Counties and a good-sized arsenal regained control of the tunnel. McCormick Company was dismissed from the project. Immigrants new to the area were recruited and paid one dollar a day, setting up "tent towns." **Wardsville**, a tent town, was closest to Rocheport. **Zanzabar** was peopled with freed blacks. **Dago City** was for the Italians and **Gillettsville** was the tent town for the Irish. P.O. 1827-now. Pop. 255.

Rock Bridge Memorial State Park (Boone). One of the important formations in this Department of Natural Resources park is a rock bridge (LI).

Rock Port (Atchison) county seat. Laid out by Nathan Meek, across the creek from Meek's mill, the name is derived from the fact that Rock Creek is rocky at this point. At one time the name was spelled as one word but in 1853 it was divided to avoid confusion with Rocheport. In 1856, the county seat moved from Linden to Rock Port (RF). Pop. 1,438.

Rockaway Beach (Taney). This is probably a promotional name, drawing on the popular beach name in New York (RF). P.O. 1933-now.

Rocky Comfort (McDonald). The oxymoronic name may reflect the nature of this place. Steep, rocky hills slope to gentle valleys. Another source suggests the name was given by a traveler who mentioned that this spot reminded him of Rocky Comfort, Arkansas (LI). Poet Dennis Murphy remembered:

> Evening Shade, Buffalo,
> Rocky Comfort, and Birch Tree—
> It matters little where I go;
> Ozark towns keep haunting me.

P.O. 1860-now.

Rolla [RAH luh] (Phelps) county seat. Local legend says this town was named after Raleigh, North Carolina, which nobody knew how to spell. A competing story goes that there was a fight over the location of the town. The winners of the location battle let the losers pick the name, and the losers did the natural thing—they named it after the mangiest dog in town. Yet another story goes that the town was named after the hero of a melodrama called "Pizarro" (RF). P.O. 1858-now. Pop. 14,090.

Romance (Ozark). For years, the post office here received valentines and love letters from folks wanting the postmark on their envelopes. The name, and its connotations, was chosen by the wife of a postmaster who gave him her list of choices (RF). P.O. 1884-1967.

Rome (Douglas). This post office was named after the city in Italy (RF). P.O. 1876-1957.

Rosati (Phelps). Joseph Rosati was the first bishop of St. Louis, honored by the 100 Italian families who settled here (VR). P.O. 1931-1966.

Round Spring (Shannon). There are hundreds of springs in the limestone-based Ozarks. Most of them have descriptive names like this one, and some come with legends about their creation. This one tells that an angry Indian chief stomped on the ground until he made this perfectly round spring, about 80 feet in diameter (APM). P.O. 1871-1894, 1927-1980.

Ruckers Prairie (Franklin). This prairie region was named for an early settler, Ambrose Rucker. The post office, which he ran, was named for him also (RF). In most Missouri places given a family name, the apostrophe (and sometimes the "s") is left out.

Rush Hill
Rushville

Rush Hill (Audrain). This farming community was named to honor two settlers named Rush and Hill (APM). P.O. 1881-now. Pop. 121.

Rushville (Buchanan). This town in Rush Township was named for the dense growth of rushes nearby (RF). P.O. 1853-now. Pop. 306.

CENTRAL OVERLAND CALIFORNIA
A N D
PIKE'S PEAK EXPRESS CO.

APRIL 8, 2009

P O N Y
EXPRESS!
FROM SAINT JOSEPH, MO.,
TO
SAN FRANCISCO
IN TEN DAYS!
(FIFTEEN DAYS DURING WINTER)

Passes through and takes letters to the following points: Fort Kearney, Fort Laramie, Fort Bridger, Great Salt Lake City, Camp Floyd, Virginia City, Placerville and Sacramento City. **CHARGES**. Letters not exceeding 1/4 oz $2 50. Letters over 1/4 oz. and not exceeding 1/2 oz. $5 00, and so on, always to be pre-paid.

S

Safe (Maries). The letters in the name stand for Shinkle, Aufderheide, Fann and Essman, four early settlers in the area.

WHEN THE SAINTS COME MARCHING IN

French Catholic tradition obliged settlers to name their cities in honor of patron saints. Because of this practice, many of our earliest settlements—Saint Louis, Saint Charles, Saint Peters, Sainte Genevieve—are so named. The reference for the saint's name is sometimes clear. It may honor the patron saint of a ruling monarch, as in the case of Saint Louis and Saint Charles. Other times, the reasons are not so clear. They may have to do with the founder's patron saints, the saint's day or other remembrance. Five Missouri rivers, four counties and at least 50 towns are named for saints.

MAY 6, 2009

Saint Charles [saynt CHAHRLZ] (St. Charles). This site on the Missouri River near the Mississippi was well known to travelers, who called it *Les Petites Cotes,* or, in English, "The Little Hills." In 1767, a Spanish fort named Fort Charles the Prince, named for Prince Charles who later became King Charles IV, was built here. This told traders that the Spanish were now in command of the river. The Spanish abandoned the fort after a year. Later, a French town was built nearby. It was called *San Carlos,* Spanish for "Saint Charles," in honor of the king's patron saint. Through usage, the name became Saint Charles. This name is unusual because the Spanish did not change the area much, so few of their early place names have lasted. P.O. 1806-now. This was Missouri's first capital and is now Missouri's seventh largest city. Pop. 54,555. *APRIL 8, 2009*

JUNE 29, 2008

Saint Charles County. This name comes from one of Missouri's original five counties, organized during territorial government. It came from the name of the settlement. Organized 1812. Pop. 212,907.

Saint Clair [saynt KLAIR] (Franklin). This town was known as Traveler's Repose until 1859 when citizens changed it to name the post office and honor an engineer of the Southwestern Branch Railroad. Traveler's Repose sounded too much like a cemetery or tavern (VR). P.O. 1859-now. Pop. 3,917.

Saint Clair County. This county, like many others, was named for a Revolutionary War hero General Arthur St. Clair; he was also the first governor of the Northwest Territory, in 1791 (RF). Organized 1841.

Saint Francis River [saynt FRAN sis]. This river is a tributary of the Mississippi River, and principal waterway in the southeastern Ozarks. It forms the east-west boundary between several counties. Known as *Cholohollay,* meaning "smoke" to the Native Americans, it may have been renamed by Pere Marquette to honor a Jesuit missionary with whom he spent time before he started his trip. Some say the river was named by early settlers or explorers for the patron saint of travelers, St. Francois of Assisi, but few, if any, of the early explorers were of that order (RF). "Francis" is the English or American version of "Francois," and the county retains the French spelling, creating considerable confusion.

Saint Francois County. The county is named after the river that runs almost entirely through it, but the county retains the French spelling. See Saint Francis River. Organized 1821. Pop. 48,904.

Saint James (Phelps). This town was first named Scioto for an Ohio (RF). The town was renamed when it prospered as a shipping point for the nearby Meramec Iron Works, owned by Thomas James, an Ohioan (VR). Because the town is named for James' name saint, it is sometimes assumed that James was Catholic. Not so. He and his family were Episcopalians (RF). P.O. 1860-now. Pop. 3,256.

Saint Joseph (Buchanan). Joseph Robidoux, a French trader, founded St. Joseph in 1840. It is named for Robidoux's patron saint with streets named for Robidoux's children. Thousands of people went west through St. Joseph when gold was discovered in California; today, the town is famous for its part in the history of the Pony Express and for its fine 19th-century architecture. It is Missouri's fifth largest city in population. P.O. 1843-now. Pop. 71,852.

Saint Louis [saynt LOO is] or [saynt LOO uhs] or [saynt LYOO is]. When this city was founded in 1764, its settlers were the citizens of French King Louis XIV. Custom required conquerors to credit patron saints for victories. St. Louis is, therefore, named for Louis IX, the patron saint of Louis XIV. After the Louisiana Purchase (1803), the streets were named like the streets of Philadelphia, early America's most important city; north-south streets were numbered and east-west streets named after trees. Nicknames include "Vide Poche" and "Mound City." The nickname "The Gateway to the West" for the landmark 630-foot stainless steel arch on the waterfront is promoted by the city. Today, St. Louis is Missouri's second largest city in population. P.O. 1804-now. Pop. 396,685.

Saint Louis County. This name comes from the city. It was given in 1812 when the county was one of the five original counties in territorial government. The city is no longer part of the county, however. In 1877, the thriving and industrial city separated its government from the surrounding less prosperous and agricultural county. Today, the county includes fine housing and business areas and is Missouri's most populated county. Pop. 993,529.

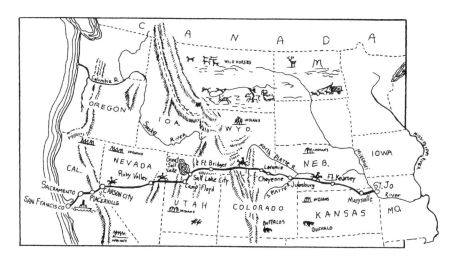

Thousands of people went west through St. Joseph when gold was discovered in California. It is also famous for its part in the history of the Pony Express.

Saint Mary
Salem

Saint Mary (Sainte Genevieve). Originally known as Camp Rowdy, when easterners came to open a store, the town became known briefly as Yankeetown. Soon it was an important shipping point, especially for St. Marys Seminary at Perryville. It gained the name Saint Marys Landing (RF). Incorporated as City of Saint Mary, the official name for post office and telephone companies is Saint Mary. Locals still say "Saint Marys" and the highway department has used both (LI). P.O. 1831-now. Pop. 461.

Saint Patrick (Clark). Settled by Irish settlers, this claims to be the only town in the world bearing the name of the Irish patron saint. It was originally to be called Marysville, but the name was already in use (APM). It is the home of an annual celebration on March 17; people often send bundles of stamped mail to the postmaster with a request for the special postmark on the holiday. P.O. 1857-1860, 1867-1869, 1878-now.

Saint Peters (St. Charles). Today, Missouri's tenth in population, the city was named for a Jesuit mission that located here in 1819. The name of the mission, and the town, was sometimes written Saint Peter's, but over time the apostrophe became optional (RF). P.O. 1841-now. Pop. 45,779.

"Saint Petersburg." When Mark Twain wrote about Hannibal, he adopted the name of the capital of the Russian empire for his "poor little shabby village" (RF).

Sainte Genevieve [saynt JEN uh veev] (Ste. Genevieve) county seat. A Catholic saint who started life as a shepherd girl in the fifth century, Ste. Genevieve is the patron saint of Paris, France. Perhaps the settlers arrived at their new home on the Mississippi River on January 3, the day given by Catholics to honor Ste. Genevieve. Or, the name may have been given in honor of an early woman settler named Genevieve. The town is a National Historic Site and important in the history of architecture, for it contains the richest collection of French Colonial buildings in the United States. P.O. 1805-now. Pop. 4,411.

Sainte Genevieve County. This name came from the settlement and was given when the county was organized in 1812. It was one of the original five Missouri counties. Organized 1812. Pop. 16,037.

Salem [SAY luhm] (Dent) county seat. This lovely old name is a version of the Hebrew *Shalom*, meaning "Peace." It has been used by towns in almost every state, and four places in Missouri. This town was first listed as Dent County Court House, but quickly appropriated Salem when Linn County's Salem went out of business. In spite of the peaceful connotations, this county seat town was at least half destroyed in the Civil War. P.O. (Benton) 1840-1847, (Hickory) 1847, (Linn) 1855-1869, (Dent) 1869-now. Pop. 4,486.

Saline County [suh LEEN]. *Saline* is French for "salty," and this county is named for its many salt springs (RF). Organized 1820. Pop. 23,523.

Saline River. Named for the French word meaning "salty," the reason for this name is somewhat in dispute. There are many salt springs and salt licks near its course (RF), but the river itself is not particularly salty.

Salt River. Called by explorer Zebulon Pike in 1805 the Ahana River, this tributary of the Mississippi River is named for its saltiness. In Missouri politics, to "row a man up Salt River" meant to defeat him or make him uncomfortable (Enc).

Salt Springs (Saline). Some say that this community was Missouri's first white settlement, as early as 1700 (VR). There are two large salt springs nearby (RF). P.O. 1875-1907.

Saltpeter Cave. There are eight caves by this name in Missouri, indicating the importance of the mineral in early years. Saltpeter is used to make gunpowder.

Sam A. Baker State Park (Wayne). Baker (1874-1933) was the 36th Missouri governor. A Republican with a Democratic Congress, most of his efforts were unsuccessful. His administration was most remarkable for its campaign to "Lift Missouri Out of the Mud," resulting in funds to pave many state roads that had been impassable in wet weather.

Sand Springs (Webster). This spot, and its town, was named because the water appears to bubble up out of sand (LI). P.O. 1863-1907.

Santa Fe (Monroe). The Texan War of Independence or Mexican War had interested Missourians, who sent many men to fight for Texas independence from Mexico. This town was founded and named in honor of Santa Fe, New Mexico (RF). P.O. 1854-now.

Santa Fe Trail, The. First opened in 1822, this wagon trail went from Missouri to Santa Fe, Mexico (now New Mexico). Mexico had just become independent from Spain and was anxious to trade with Americans. Americans took factory-made skillets, hammers, mirrors and cloth; they purchased mules and donkeys and brought back silver (DM).

Santiago (Benton). The man who laid out this town had fought in the 1898 Battle of Santiago (in Cuba) during the Spanish-American War.

Santuzza [san tuh ZAY] (Lewis). This post office name and its unusual pronunciation is a mystery (RF). P.O. 1899-1902.

Sarcoxie [sahr KAHK see] (Jasper). First called Centerville for its location on Center Creek, the name was changed to honor an old Shawnee chief who lived nearby. The meaning of the name was "rising sun" (Enc). P.O. 1838-now. Pop. 1,330.

Sardine (Cooper). The elderly Dean was always grumpy, giving him the nickname "Sorry Dean." His nickname got stuck on the little town, which consisted of a general store, blacksmith shop, stage stop and several homes (APM).

Sarvis Point (Webster). "Sarvis" was the pioneer name for the serviceberry plant (LI), which grew thick around this post office (RF).

Savannah (Andrew) county seat. Take your choice from the opinions of experts. The town was named for: (1) Savannah, Georgia (VR); (2) the first white child born in the town, Savannah Woods, who was in turn named for her father's hometown in Georgia (RF). The first county seat was White Hall, but was moved to Savannah in 1841. P.O. 1841-now. Pop. 4,352.

Schuyler County [SKEYE luhr]. This, the second smallest county in the state, is named after General Philip Schuyler, a hero in the Revolutionary War (RF). Organized 1843. Pop. 4,236.

Scotland County [SKAHT luhnd]. The county was a part of the hunting grounds allotted by the government to Native Americans and was known as headquarters of the Chief Keokuk (1780-1848) of the Sauk and the Fox. It was named by Scottish settlers for their home (RF). Organized 1841. Pop. 4,822.

Scott City [SKAHT] (Scott). First called North Star, the town changed its name when Margaret Scott built her home here (LI). P.O. 1960-now. Pop. 4,292.

Scott County. This county was named for Honorable John Scott (1782-1861), the first congressman from Missouri (RF). He was a supporter of Thomas Hart Benton and is credited with helping secure the final votes to elect Benton as first U.S. senator (DM). See Benton. Organized 1821. Pop. 39,376.

Sedalia [suh DAYL yuh] (Pettis). In 1852, George R. Smith convinced the Pacific Railroad to divert its course and cross the prairie. Five years later, he bought 1,000 acres along the new right-of-way and platted a town, which he named Sedville, using the nickname, Sed, of his daughter Sarah. Later, realizing that the village was growing to city size and could use a more sophisticated name, he changed it to the classical-sounding Sedalia (VR). The name has been adopted in fifteen states, nine to the east and six to the west. Because settlement generally moves west, it's very unusual for names to move eastward (RF). Sedalia is home to the Missouri State Fair and is famous as the terminus of the Texas longhorn cattle drives (BD). If you've seen the movie *Rawhide*, you'll recall Clint Eastwood was driving his cattle towards Sedalia (LI). P.O. 1861-now. Pop. 19,800.

Seelitz (Perry). This community was started as an offshoot of the original Perry County German Lutheran communities (see Altenburg). The name probably came from the leader's first parish in Germany (RF).

Seligman [SEL ig muhn] (Barry). First named Roller's Ridge, the name was changed to honor a New York banker who never saw the place. He purchased stock to build the Frisco Railroad through the county, and also donated money to build a nondenominational church. Baptists, Methodists and Christians enjoyed the building (APM). P.O. 1880-now. Pop. 593.

Senath [SEE nuhth] (Dunklin). This unusual name was given for the wife, Senath Douglass, of first postmaster, A.W. Douglass (RF). P.O. 1881-now. Pop. 1,622.

Seneca [SEN uh kuh] (Newton). This town was named for the Seneca nation. Members lived across the state line in Indian Territory (RF). P.O. 1869-now. Pop. 1,885.

Seven Mile Bend
Shadow Rock

Seven Mile Bend (Pemiscot County). This large bend in Pemiscot Bayou is named for the length of the curve (RF).

Seven Mile Creek (Audrain and Callaway). This creek is named for its length (RF).

Seven Mile Island (Dunklin). In the St. Francis River, this is named for its approximate distance from Kennett (RF).

Seven Points Hills (Oregon). These seven small hills are clustered near Thomasville (numerologists take note: It's near the Eleven-Point River!) (RF).

Seven Springs (Dallas). The name is taken from the number of springs; the place is also called Fifteen Springs for the same reason (RF).

Seven Star Springs (Barry). These springs are arranged like the seven stars. They were earlier called Hodo Mineral Springs (RF).

Seven Stone Arches Bridge (St. Francois). This was the winning name in a 1940 contest to name the recently completed bridge. The bridge has seven stone arches (RF).

Seventysix (Perry). This village grew up around a river landing on the banks of the Mississippi River. There are several stories about the name: (1) A steamboat captain went to rescue people in the great flood of 1844. He made 76 trips (RF). (2) A steamboat captain decided to quit swearing by substituting the exclamation, "That beats all 76." Apparently, this landing was particularly difficult and he used the phrase so often that his men got in the habit of calling it Seventysix (RF). (3) The Government River Commission gave the name when it numbered the river landings and this one was . . . (RF). (4) The name came from Seventy-six, Kentucky, in turn named in commemoration of the Declaration of Independence (GS). P.O. 1880-1954.

Seymour (Webster). This town was named after Seymour, Indiana, by a railroad man (RF). P.O. 1881-now. Pop. 1,636.

Shadow Rock (Taney). This is a large bluff and rock that casts a shadow over Swan Creek near Forsyth.

Shake Rag (Monroe). This African American settlement was named to mock the settlers; the name suggests the bobbing of bandannas worn around the head and knotted (RF).

Shake Rag (Warren). Named to make fun of the ragged clothes of the early European settlers, this is one of the oldest place names in the county and probably started as a derisive nickname (RF).

Shamrock (Callaway). The town was probably settled by Irish, but some say the name came from a huge rock. The rock, supposedly, was a meeting place and a place to leave messages and mail. P.O. 1833-1861, 1863-1954.

Shanghai (Johnson). An early settler here raised Shanghai chickens (RF).

Shanghai (Vernon). Two suggestions: This early town was reputedly a drinking and brawling place, like the celebrated city in China, OR, the name may signify a type of shanty cabin constructed with boards nailed up and down rather than horizontally (RF).

Shannon County [SHAN uhn]. George F. Shannon of Marion County was a member of the Lewis and Clark Expedition in 1804 and later became U.S. attorney general. He barely escaped death when he got separated from the party while looking for two horses (RF). Organized 1841. Pop. 7,613.

Sharp (Ozark). This town was named for a trader who was keen enough to get the better of others. P.O. 1890-1915.

Shelbina [shel BEYE nuh] (Shelby). This town was named for the county namesake, Isaac Shelby. See Shelby County. P.O. 1858-now. Pop. 2,172.

Shelby County [SHEL bee]. Because most of the settlers were from Kentucky, the county was named for Kentucky Governor Isaac Shelby (1750-1826) who served three terms there (1792-1796, 1812-1816, 1816-1820). Governor Shelby fought in the Revolutionary War, and also served in the legislature of Carolina (RF). Organized 1835. Pop. 6,942.

Shelbyville (Shelby) county seat. Named for Shelby County, this town, just north of the geographic center of the county, was used as a Union headquarters during the Civil War. The Shelbyville Stockade was built of 15-foot, heavy oak posts sharpened at the upper ends and built around the courthouse (RF). See Shelby County. P.O. 1836-now. Pop. 582.

Sheldon (Vernon). (1) This town was laid out by Sheldon A. Wight, a large landowner, and given his name (RF). (2) See Adrian. P.O. 1881-now. Pop. 464.

Shell Knob (Barry). One source asserts that this knob was named for the shell fossils found therein (RF); another says it was named for Mr. Schell, an early trading post owner (LI). P.O. 1872-now.

Shepherd of the Hills Homestead (Taney). This was originally the isolated homestead of John and Charles Ross, who are Old Matt and Young Matt in the sentimental novel The Shepherd of the Hills. Promoters have turned the site into a theatre and theme park. Here you'll find "Inspiration Tower," a 230'10" concrete observation deck with a view of the Ozarks. "There is no other concrete tower like this in the world," boast the ads.

Shibboleth [shi BOH luhth] (Washington). This mining center was home of John Smith, a man with a common name. He called himself John Smith T (Tennessee) to separate himself from the crowd. His longing for an unusual name is reflected in the name he gave his village. *Shibboleth* is a Hebrew word meaning "flood" or "stream"; it was used as a password by the Gileadites (RF).

"Shoofly" (Clay). This nickname was given to Prathersville because the little town was so small.

Sibley [SIB lee] (Jackson). The town was named for Fort Sibley, a fort commanded by George Sibley from 1818 to 1826. William Clark, of Lewis and Clark fame, first noted the site in June 1804, when passing by here with the Corps of Discovery Expedition. He noted the prominent hilltop position and called it "Fort Point" in his journals. He returned in 1808 to oversee its construction. First named Fort Clark, then Fort Osage, then Fort Sibley, it lasted until 1826—longer than any other Missouri fort. P.O. 1842-1864, 1866-now. Pop. 367.

Sikeston [SEYEK stuhn] (Scott). Platted by John Sikes in 1860 (VR), this town is known for its lighted Christmas displays and Lambert's Cafe, "home of throwed rolls." At Lambert's, extra portions of home-style foods are brought from table to table and fresh, hot rolls are "throwed" to diners. P.O. 1860-1864, 1867-now. Pop. 17,641.

Silva [SIL vuh] (Wayne). (1) *Silva* is the Latin word for "tree" or "forest," so this name designates a location in woods (LI). (2) The name was given by a postmistress for the name of her friend Silvia; it was spelled to reflect local pronunciation (RF). P.O. 1902-now.

Silver Dollar City (Taney). While this theme park name suggests good old-fashioned value, it also has roots in history. In the early 1800s, the Yoachum family began coining a silver dollar for local currency. They said it was cast from silver found in the family mine. The truth is the moonshining family cast the dollars from silver paid by neighboring Delaware Indians for liquor, who received the silver as government payments. Supplying liquor to the Indians was illegal, and the moonshiners concocted the mine story to bury the facts. In the 1830s, when government came to the Ozarks, the mine "caved in" and was "lost," adding to the notable number of "lost silver mines" remembered in Ozark legend and lore (LI).

Silver Mine (Madison). The only silver mine in Missouri operated here. The source was two thin veins and the mine was soon closed (LI).

Singing Waters (Buchanan). Tradition says that this lyrically named waterway was named by a lost Native American girl who thought there was a familiar song in its waters and falls. She visited here while looking for her lost home (RF).

Six Crossing Hollow
or **Old Deer Crossing** (Texas). Nine miles north of Hazelton, this crossing was named by old rafters who saw a large herd of deer here (GA).

Six Flags Over Mid-America (Franklin). This amusement park was built by a Texas corporation that first built Six Flags Over Texas and took its name from the six governments of Texas during its history. The name fits in Missouri if you count our political affiliations this way: French (1719-1763), Spanish (1763-1800), French (1800-1803), American (1803-Civil War), Missouri (part of Civil War), American (end of Civil War to the present).

Slabtown Springs (Texas). Four miles north of Hazelton on the Big Piney, this town was named for its mountains of lumber ready for transport (GA).

Slater (Saline). This town was named for Colonel John F. Slater of Chicago, director of the Chicago and Alton Railroad (RF). P.O. 1878-now. Pop. 2,186.

Sleeper (Laclede). This town was named for a construction gang foreman (his name, not his work style) (RF). P.O. 1883-1955.

Sligo Furnace [SLEYE goh] (Dent). This iron company town, once home to 300 families, was named for the Sligo Iron Company of St. Louis (RF). The name was shortened to Sligo in 1887, after Crawford County's Sligo post office closed. P.O. Sligo Furnace 1882-1887, Sligo 1887-1966.

Sligo (Crawford). This town was named for one in Ireland, probably by homesick immigrants. P.O. 1880-1886.

Smackout (Boone). A story tells that this name was given for the store owner who would explain to irritated customers that he was just "smackout" of most of the things on their lists (RF).

Smithton (Pettis). This common town name has been found in three other Missouri counties, but lasted longest in Pettis, where George Smith was a prominent figure (see Sedalia). Smith, called "Father of Pettis County," was important in keeping Missouri in the Union and many county places were named for him or his family. P.O. (Boone) 1820-1821, (Gentry) 1858-1861, (Worth) 1861-1867, 1869-1870, (Pettis) 1871-now. Pop. 532.

Smithville (Clay). The first settler here was Humphrey Smith, born in New Jersey and known as Yankee Smith (APM). P.O. 1844-now. Pop. 2,525.

Sniabar River [SNEYE uh bahr] (Lafayette). Two opinions: (1) Also written Sni-A-Bar, this sluggish river was wide and slow enough to confuse navigators. They could actually get turned around. When the channel was closed by broken rafts or driftwood, boatmen called it Barred Sni or Sni Barred (CG). (2) When pronounced, the French word *chenal* (meaning "channel") sounds sort of like "sneye"; *chenal* followed by the name Hubert, for resident French merchant Antoine Hubert, may be the phonetic source of the name (RF).

Snibar (Lafayette). The post office was named for the river. P.O. 1847-1879.

Solo [SOH loh] (Texas). The storekeeper named this place for its remote location (RF).

South Fork (Howell). Originally named Cross Roads, this town is located on the headwaters of West Fork of the South Fork of Spring River (RF). P.O. 1860-1867, 1875-1960. Pop. 80.

Southwest City (McDonald). This is the southwesternmost town in Missouri, where Missouri joins Oklahoma and Arkansas. P.O. 1871-now. Pop. 600.

Spanish Fort (Lawrence). This high place has the appearance of a fort, and local tradition asserts that DeSoto built one here and used it (RF).

Spanish Lake (St. Louis). First known as Rich Valley, this lake was used in the 1790s by the Spanish governor as a resort. It was also called Spanish Pond (RF). P.O. 1880-1900.

Sparta (Christian). This store and town was named after Sparta, Tennessee (APM). P.O. 1876-now. Pop. 751.

Speed (Cooper). This town was first called New Palestine, resulting in its mail being missent to New Palestine, Texas. The name was changed to honor a conductor on the railroad (his name, not his work style) (RF).

Spickard (Grundy). Incorporated as Spickardsville, this town was located on land belonging to George A. Spickard. In 1893, the thrifty post office eliminated "sville," thus saving ink. The little town drew national attention in the 1890s when women of the church destroyed a saloon with their hatchets, and were taken to trial by the saloon owner. The trial drew 1,200 spectators (LI). P.O. Spickardsville 1872-1892, Spickard 1893-now. Pop. 326.

Springfield (Greene) county seat. There are different stories about the naming, somewhat depending on audience. (1) The name choice was put to a vote of all citizens (landowning white males). James Wilson, who had been born and raised in Springfield, Massachusetts, put up a tent near the voting booth where he offered voters a sip of white whiskey and gave them a pep talk about his favorite name (RF). (2) Name story (1) is not shared with school children. They will tell you the place is named for a spring discovered by pioneers in a field. Nicknamed "The Queen City of the Ozarks" (KM), our third most populous town is best known for Bass Pro Shop and Springfield-style cashew chicken. P.O. 1834-now. Pop. 140,494.

Springfield Plateau. A large flat land in the midst of the rocky Ozarks, farmers here found the terrain more fertile, less rocky and more easily worked than the nearby hills (VR).

Spy Mound (Bates). When abolitionist John Brown lived in the territory, he and his followers went to this limestone mound to watch for enemies. From the summit, a viewer can see for 12 miles in all directions (APM).

Stanberry (Gentry). The town was named for John Stanberry, an early settler. P.O. 1879-now. Pop. 1,310.

Stark City (Newton). This town was named for William Stark, a successful nursery man, for his large nursery there. P.O. 1912-now. Pop. 127.

Starkenburg (Montgomery). A limestone church and its grounds is a focal point for this community. It was named by the first priest, in honor of a castle near his ancestral home in Germany.

Steelville (Crawford). First named Davey, this town was renamed for James Steel, an early settler here. The name seemed especially appropriate when high-grade iron ore was discovered and the town became a center for miners and their paychecks (VR). P.O. 1836-now. Pop. 1,465.

Stella (Newton). First called the Village of Springs, this fisherman's paradise was renamed after Stella Eagle, the granddaughter of a founder. P.O. 1884-now. Pop. 132.

Sterling Price Community Lake (Chariton). This Department of Conservation property is named for the nearby home of the Democratic governor (1853-1857) and Confederate general (LI).

Stewartsville (DeKalb). Robert Stewart was one of the leaders in building the Hannibal and St. Joseph line, the first railroad to cross the state. Elected governor from 1857-1861, he is remembered for his eccentricity. One good story: Returning home one evening, he rode his horse into the governor's mansion and fed it oats from a silver bowl on the buffet. Pop. 732.

Stockton (Cedar) county seat. First named Lancaster, the name was changed to honor John C. Fremont (the Pathfinder), who was credited with saving California during the Mexican War. See Fremont. When he became unpopular for his actions during the Civil War, the people petitioned the legislature to change the name to Stockton, in honor of Commodore Richard Stockton. Stockton is now the gateway town for visitors to Stockton State Park and recreational Stockton Lake, formed by construction of a controversial dam that buried many small villages. P.O. 1859-now. Pop. 1,579.

Stoddard County [STAH dard]. This county was named in honor of Amos Stoddard (1762-1813), agent of the U.S. government who received the transfer of the Louisiana Territory from France (RF). Organized 1835. Pop. 28,895.

Stone County [STOHN]. This county was named not for its principle soil component but for John W. Stone. He was an early settler from Tennessee and an influential member of the Taney County community. Stone and Taney Counties have had deep ties since their beginnings. Both are benefitting from Branson tourism (LI). Organized 1851. Pop. 19,078.

Stringtown (Cole). There have been at least twelve places called Stringtown in Missouri—places where houses and stores were lined up along the road.

Sturgeon
Sunset

When the post office insisted that every town name be unique, the Cole County town snapped up the name. Unlike crossroad towns, stringtowns depended on one road for transportation and success. This weakness put most of them out of business as new roads were built. P.O. 1857-1860, 1864-1882. Pop. 50.

Sturgeon [STUHR juhn] (Boone). When it was announced that the railroad was coming to this spot, the citizens of nearby Buena Vista moved their houses, creating an instant village of 150 people. It was thought that the overly large Boone County would be split in two, and this would be the seat of the new county (to be called Rollins). Plans never developed, and the town, named after Isaac H. Sturgeon, North Missouri Railroad superintendent, languished (APM). P.O. 1857-now. Pop. 838.

Sublette (Adair). Named for a prominent family. P.O. 1868-now.

Success (Texas). When the Hastings store owner found an unusual spring near his place, he decided to make a resort, giving it the hopeful name Success. It was not successful. Residents moved to a better location when two nearby highways came together in a "Y." The new town was called Wye City, but the post office kept the old name. P.O. 1880-now. Pop. 130.

Sullivan (Franklin). This town was named for Stephen and Dorcas Sullivan, landowners who gave land to the Frisco Railroad when it was coming through. P.O. 1860-now. Pop. 5,551.

Sullivan County [SUH luh vuhn]. This was named by Honorable E.C. Morelock for his native county in Tennessee. Organized 1845. Pop. 6,326.

Sumner (Chariton). This town, named after a civil engineer, calls itself "the goose capital of the world." It is the location of Maxi, the world's largest Canada goose, modeled in concrete. P.O. 1883-now. Pop. 140.

Sunkland. See Swampeast.

Sunklands, The (Texas). This huge old sinkhole, reminder of an ancient cave system, is part of the Department of Conservation holdings at Burr Oak Basin.

Sunset (Polk). This name was given in memory of an incident, or from one of the seven other Sunsets in the United States (RF). P.O. 1888-1900.

"Swampeast Missouri." The Bootheel has had many nicknames, including this one given for its wet marshes. The presently excellent farmland, used to grow rice (among other crops), was the home of giant trees and water moccasins until the swamps were drained and a canal system put in place. The name Swampeast was popularized by writer and activist Thad Snow in his writings about Mississippi County. Another nickname was "Sunkland."

Swan (Taney). This place name appears several places in the Ozarks. It may have come from an early family by that name (RF). P.O. 1880-1957.

Swan Creek (Taney). This creek was named for its resident bird (LI).

Swashing Creek. The French *Joachim*, when spoken by Americans, can sound like "swashing" (GS). See Joachim Creek.

Swedeborg (Pulaski). This was a Swedish settlement, laid out by the Swede Company (RF). P.O. 1881-now.

Sweden (Douglas). The townspeople wanted their town named Sweten, after a settler, but they spelled the name wrong (RF).

Sweet Springs (Saline). Originally named Brownsville, the name was changed partly because there were 25 Brownsvilles in the United States (LI). As "Saratoga of the West," this town and its springs were known for its 400-guest hotel, built in 1876 by the Marmadukes. It was later used as Marmaduke Military Academy, but abandoned when the building burned (APM). P.O. 1840-now. Pop. 1,595.

Swiss (Gasconade). Many people in this town were from Switzerland (RF).

Tabo Creek [TAB oh]. This name could be an American version of the French *terre beau*, or *terre bonne*, meaning "beautiful earth" or "good earth" (VR). Or, it may be the English spelling of the personal name Tabeau, a French trapper who settled on the creek (CG). In Lafayette County, a post office took the name from 1847 to 1899.

Tamerlane Bend. This is where the steamboat *Tamerlane* blew up and sank in 1848 (CG).

Taney County [TAY nee]. This is the only county in the United States to be named for Chief Justice Roger Taney of the U.S. Supreme Court (RF). When in office, the Maryland native issued the Dred Scott decision. Today, thanks to country music and tourism, this is one of the fastest-growing counties in the state (LI). Organized 1837. Pop. 25,561.

Taneycomo (Taney). The lake, and the town, are named for the abbreviation of Taney County, Missouri (LI). P.O. 1919-now.

Taos [TOWS] or [TAH uhs] (Cole). First named Haarville, for an early German settler, Taos was renamed after Missourians came home from the Spanish-American War (RF). P.O. 1848-1907. Pop. 802.

Tarkio River [TAHR kee oh]. A tributary of the Missouri River, this name is somewhat of a mystery. Some experts say it means "difficult to ford" in a Native American language (JL). Others say it means "walnut" (LI). A town in Atchison County bears the name. P.O. 1843-1845, 1849-1856, 1863-1864, 1880-now.

Taum Sauk Mountain [TAHM SUHK] (Iron). At 1,772 feet above sea level, this is the highest peak in Missouri. It was probably named for the Sauk tribe. *Taum* may be a variation of the Sauk word *tongo*, meaning "big." See also Mina Sauk.

Taylor (Marion). This town takes its name from a mill owned by John Taylor in the mid- 1800s. P.O. 1873-now.

Tebbetts (Callaway). This railroad station and farming community at the edge of the Missouri River floodplain was named for an official of the Chicago and Alton Railroad. P.O. 1895-now.

Tecumseh [tuh KUHM suh] (Ozark). This town was named for Tecumseh (1768-1813), a Shawnee chief who traveled among the Delawares, Shawnees and Cherokees who had come to the Spanish territory and settled along the St. Francis and White Rivers. He spoke for unity among the tribes and against the white men. His oratory combined reminders of the great religious, cultural and military traditions of the tribes with a plea for abstinence from liquor (LI). The Shawnee believed that a meteor called Tecumtha was a fiery panther blazing across the sky. Tecumseh was born on a night when meteors fell (JL).

Ten Mile Pond (Mississippi). Settlers guessed that this lake was about ten miles long. Today, its length has been reduced by drainage canals (RF).

Teresita [ter uh SEYE tuh] (Shannon). After his first choice, Pleasant Grove, was rejected, the postmaster took suggestions. A postal employee told him *teresita* meant "spot on the earth." In truth, it is Spanish for "little Teresa," the name for a girl (RF).

Texas County
Tiff

Texas County [TEK suhs]. This county was first named Ashley County for William Ashley, a fur trader and miner who was elected first lieutenant general of the state and who traded in the area. See Ashley Cave. The name was officially changed to Texas County. Many men from here joined Doniphan on his march to Texas. See Doniphan. Others went with Stephen Austin to settle Texas (RF). Locals speculate the name is appropriate since this is the largest county in Missouri (LI). Organized 1845. Pop. 21,476.

Thayer (Oregon). The town was named for a railroad boss. P.O. 1884-now. Pop. 1,996.

Theodosia [thee uh DOH shee uh] (Ozark). This post office was named for the wife of the first postmaster. P.O. 1886-1951. Pop. 235.

Thomas Hill (Randolph). This small post office was named for an early settler, William Thomas, and was located on a hill (RF). P.O. 1874-1902.

Thomas Hill Reservoir (Randolph and Macon). Developed by the Associated Electric Cooperative, it is named for the defunct town.

Thompson (Audrain). The spelling of the name of this agricultural community has been in dispute. It was spelled Tompson but the post office puts in the "h" (VR). The first postmaster spelled his name with the "h" (RF). P.O. 1883-now.

Three Creeks State Forest (Boone). After Emancipation, 100 former slaves and their families homesteaded here, and found the rocky terrain better for hunting than farming (LI). Today it is managed by the Department of Conservation. The three creeks are Bass, Turkey and Grindstone (LI).

Three Mound Prairie (Polk). This small prairie has three mounds (RF).

Three Notch Road. The first road in Missouri was built between Mine La Motte and Ste. Genevieve. In its first days, the road was simply a path through the woods. To follow it, a traveler would look for trees with three cuts, or notches, on the trunk. These marked the road and its name (RF).

Tiff (Washington). This post office and shipping point is named for a miner's term for barite, originally thought to be waste to the lead miners. Later, barite was mined for its own sake (LI). P.O. 1905-now.

Tiff City (McDonald). Barite rock was common here, and gave a special character to a spring which briefly became famous for its medicinal waters. P.O. 1877-now.

Tightwad (Henry). The store owner here was such a wheeler-dealer he couldn't keep himself from making deals. After selling an exceptional watermelon to the wagon-driving mailman, who said he'd come back for it, the storekeeper sold the same melon to a city fellow in a car. The storekeeper picked another from his patch, then tried to make a switch. Discovering the trickery, the mail man shouted "Tightwad! Tightwad!" The word echoed across the valley as he drove away (LI). Sometimes this story is told using a chicken in place of a watermelon (LI). Pop. 50.

Tin Mountain (Madison). In 1870, a speculator announced that he had found tin here. He sold the land to investors who built a furnace, sunk mining shafts and brought in 1,500 people. An estimated $200,000 was sunk in the project. It was a hoax; no tin was found (RF).

Tina [TEYE nuh] (Carroll). Named for the daughter of E.M. Gilchrist, a railroad man, the unusual pronunciation has seemingly always been that way. The Tina community built a hall where there are old-time dances, with a variety of fiddlers and musicians providing the music. P.O. 1884-now. Pop. 199.

Tipton (Moniteau). The town is named for Tipton Sealey, who donated the land for the town site (RF). P.O. 1858-now. Pop. 2,026.

Toad-a-Loop [TOHD uh LOOP] (Jackson). First called Tour-de-Loup, from the French meaning "wolf's track," the name has been changed through usage to these nonsense syllables.

Toga (Stoddard). This old settlement was named for Toga Bill Rhodes, who lived there (RF). P.O. 1900-1903.

Tommy Creek (Polk). This is a short version of the original Tomahawk Creek, named for the discovery of a tomahawk here (RF).

Tower Rock (Perry). Named for the way it juts out of the Mississippi River, this dominating limestone rock was designated a National Landmark by President Ulysses S. Grant (LI).

Trail of Tears State Park. The park includes a portion of the Trail of Tears used by the Cherokees and other civilized tribes in their forced march from Tennessee to Oklahoma.

Tranquility (Clark). Scholars call this an "ideal" name; the post office lasted only a year. P.O. 1901-1902.

Treasure Island (Dunklin). This residential area in the boggy bootheel took advantage of a bit of solid ground in the swamp. Most of the year, residents traveled in and out of the area in johnboats.

Treloar (Warren). Treloar was named after William Treloar, a former teacher at Hardin College in Mexico, Missouri. He was also the first Republican elected to the Ninth Congressional district (BD). P.O. 1897-now.

Trenton (Grundy) county seat. Originally known as Bluff Grove, the town was renamed, probably for Trenton, New Jersey (VR). P.O. Bluff Grove 1840-1842, Trenton 1842-now. Pop. 6,129.

Triplett (Chariton). The town was named for the first settlers to build a house here. It is known today for goose and duck hunting, being located in the Chariton River bottoms. P.O. 1875-now. Pop. 58.

Trowel (Bollinger). This town was established by members of the Masonic Lodge, and named for their symbol (RF).

Troy (Lincoln) county seat. This town is on the site of a fort built during the War of 1812. It was known as Wood's Fort until at least 1820. Locals assert that it was renamed by a settler for Troy (Vermont) or Troy (New York). The name is quite popular in the United States; all namesakes go back to the Greek (RF). See Antioch. P.O. 1823-now. Pop. 3,811.

Truman Reservoir. Named for Harry S Truman, president and Missouri favorite son (see Lamar), the building of the dam and lake was disputed, because it took out much fine agricultural land and many people's homes.

Truxton [TRUHK stuhn] (Lincoln). Some people say this town was named for the truck wagons that came through. More likely, it was named for Captain Thomas Truxton, a naval officer in the American Revolution (LI). P.O. 1854-now. Pop. 90.

Tunas (Dallas). This interesting old name is a mystery. P.O. 1893-now.

Turkey Neck Bend (Pulaski). This dangerous bend in the Big Piney River is near the mouth of Baldridge Creek. (1) It was named for the numerous flocks of wild turkeys here (GA). (2) The bend doubles back like a turkey neck (LI).

Turnback Creek or **Turnback River** (Lawrence, Dade, Cedar). It is no small matter to locals that a place name researcher published imperfect information regarding this place name. The waterway was named, the researcher said, after pioneers camped here in the winter of 1830. Some of the party turned back, returning (it was written) to Tennessee. Not so! say the locals. The group only went back 20 miles—to Springfield (LI).

Tuscumbia [tuhs KUHM bee yuh] (Miller) county seat. This town may have been named for a Chickasaw tribal chief Tash-ka-ambi (meaning "warrior who kills") or, more likely, for the Alabama town that is his namesake (RF). P.O. 1837-now. Pop. 148.

Twelve Mile Creek (Madison). The headwaters of this creek are 12 miles from the county seat, Fredericktown.

Twin Groves (Jasper). This town is named for the very obvious twin tree groves on the prairie here. P.O. 1874-1878.

Two-Mile Prairie (Boone). Named for its average width (LI). Named for its length (RF).

Tyler (Pemiscot). The southeasternmost town in Missouri, this is situated where Missouri joins Tennessee and Arkansas. It was named for a prominent landowner and saw mill operator. P.O. 1891-now.

Tywappidy (Cape Girardeau). See Tywappity Bottoms. P.O. 1807-1811 (estimated).

Tywappity Bottoms (Scott). This name is very old, and probably harks back to a Native American word; it appears on old maps, sometimes spelled Zewapeta. Many explanations have been given. (1) In Shawnee, elk were called *wapiti*, literally "white rump" (JL). (2) *Ty* in Shawnee means "chief" (RF). (3) The Shawnee name means "place of no return," perhaps signifying that it was halfway between two important places (GS). (4) A modern nickname is pronounced [teye WOP] with this interesting explanation: This comes from railroad times, and the name is a pronounciation of the main activity in the area—this is where people whopped railroad ties from the timber (LI).

Tzi-Sho Prairie (Barton). This public land of the Department of Conservation was named to honor a branch of the Osage tribe.

U

Union. This name in Missouri usually has nothing to do with the Civil War. In fact, it most often refers to settlement of a local argument and is a hopeful name signifying that people will get along in the future.

Union (Franklin) county seat. The name is an ideal name, and one of the most popular in the United States (RF). It was given after a dispute over the location of the county seat (LI). A commission was appointed to find the center of Franklin County and establish a county seat within three miles. Newport, the original county seat, was too far west after new county boundaries were drawn (VR). P.O. 1827-now. Pop. 5,909.

Union Mill (Clinton). This mill town was located where Buchanan and Clinton Counties came together, hence the name (APM).

Union Star (DeKalb). This county was strongly Republican and pro-Union, and the town probably took this name for that reason (RF). P.O. 1863-now. Pop. 432 .

Unionville (Putnam) county seat. Situated near the Iowa state line, this town is in one of the counties split by the dispute with Iowa over the border's location (LI). Before the split, Putnam and Dodge Counties were both in Missouri. After the split, Dodge became part of Iowa. Then there was dispute in locating the Putnam County seat. Finally, this site was chosen, and the citizens consented to call it Harmony. Soon, the name was in dispute and again changed. Unionville sounded agreeable and hopeful to people worn out from argument (RF). According to some local sources, the name was adopted because the community had Union sympathies during the Civil War (LI). P.O. 1854-now. Pop. 1,989.

University City (St. Louis). A neighborhood of St. Louis, this began as a planned community; the developers wanted universities here. Washington University obliged (RF). Pop. 40,087.

Urbana [uhr BAN uh] (Dallas). A pioneer doctor named Andrews was honored with the original town name Andersonville; the name was changed to that of his Illinois home (RF). P.O. 1856-now. Pop. 350.

Valles Mines (Jefferson). The Valles family developed mines here in the late 1790s (GS).

Van Buren (Carter) county seat. This is the principal town for visitors to Ozark National Scenic Riverways National Park and has long been a county seat, first for Ripley County and now for Carter County, carved from Ripley (VR). The courthouse is the only Missouri courthouse built from cobblestones (MO). P.O. 1834-now. Pop. 893.

Van Meter State Park (Saline). This park was owned by the Van Meter family. Once the home of prehistoric Indian tribes, the site is believed to have been inhabited by Indians as early as 10,000 B.C. It contains a large Missouri Indian earthwork known locally as the Old Fort (LI).

Vandalia [van DAYL yuh] (Audrain). Named for Vandalia, Illinois, by founders that included Amos Ladd (Enc). See Laddonia. P.O. 1871-now. Pop. 2,683.

Vastus (Butler). This town was named by a schoolmaster who worked to get a post office located here. He explained that the name was Latin for "great," because "we thought we were great then and had great possibilities" (RF). Actually, the word translates to "empty," or "desolate."

Venice [VEN uhs] (Shannon). This town was named by the postmaster's son after he had read about Venice. A post office in Callaway also claimed the name, from 1895-1907. P.O. 1913-1933.

Venus (Maries). This town was named for a girl, Venus Riley (RF). P.O. 1912-1932.

Vera Cruz [VEE ruh KROOZ] (Douglas). This town was named shortly after the Mexican War (1846-1849) and named for a city in Mexico. P.O. 1859-1869, 1873-1879, 1881.

Vernon County [VUHR nuhn]. This county was named for Miles Vernon, a soldier in the War of 1812 under Andrew Jackson. He resided here, served in the state senate, and joined the Confederate Army in the Civil War. Organized 1851. Pop. 19,041.

Versailles [vuhr SAYLZ] (Morgan) county seat. (1) The town was named for Versailles, Kentucky, by settlers who brought the pronunciation with them (LI). (2) The town was named for the palace of Louis XIV near Paris, France (RF), but through usage given the American pronunciation. P.O. 1835-now. Pop. 2,365.

Viburnum [veye BUHR nuhm] (Iron). Named for the Viburnum Trend District, a narrow, 35-mile-long strip of ore in southeast Missouri, almost all of the state's lead output is today from this area. The word *viburnum* is Latin for "the wayfaring tree." It is used for a wild variety of honeysuckle that grows profusely in this area (LI). P.O. 1903-1955. Pop. 743.

Vichy [VUSH ee] or [VEE shee] (Maries). This town is named for the French resort (VR). It is named for its mineral springs, similar to those in Vichy, France (RF). P.O. 1880-now. Pop. 611.

"Vide Poche" or **"Empty Pocket"** (St. Louis). There are a variety of speculative explanations for Carondelet's unusual French nickname: (1) The inhabitants were so poor, that they had no money to pay for bread—they had empty pockets. (2) The inhabitants were skillful gamblers. If you went there for sport, you would come back with empty pockets. Americans changed the French pronunciation of *vide poche* to "wheat bush" and also used the nickname "sugar-loaf." This apparently referred to a loaf-shaped Indian mound at the south border of St. Louis near Carondelet (RF).

Vienna [veye EN uh] (Maries) county seat. (1) The founder called the village "Vi-anny" after his daughter's name (Vianna), and later mapmakers and government agencies re-spelled the name to reflect the name of the city on the Danube (LI). (2) Dr. E.G. Latham, presiding judge of the county court, wanted to name this town in honor of a deceased relative, Anna, combined with the French word *vie* meaning life. But Vie Anna was rejected by the townspeople, and Vienna was the compromise (VR). (3) It was named by German-speaking settlers for the European town, a cultural and economic center of the 19th and early 20th centuries (LI). P.O. 1856-now. Pop. 611.

Virgil City (Cedar and Vernon). Virgil Kimball and a partner laid out this county-line town. The post office roosted in Cedar County from 1867 to 1868, then Vernon County for an unknown period, then returned to Cedar County until 1876, then Vernon for an unknown period, then Cedar to 1889, then to Vernon, where it died in 1905.

Vulcan (Iron). A railroad and mining town in the historic mining district of the eastern Ozarks, it supplied the Vulcan Iron Works in St. Louis with iron. Volcanus is the Roman god of fire. P.O. 1895, 1913-now.

Waco [WAY koh] (Jasper). This town was probably named for the Texas town, because there was a great deal of trade between this region and that one (RF). P.O. 1878-now. Pop. 86.

Wah-Kon-Tah Prairie. This property of the Department of Conservation was named for the Osage name for the Deity. There is dispute whether the name means something like "creator" or "life spirit" or "almighty." Because earliest diaries and journals that mention the name were written by Europeans, the writers brought their own understanding to the meaning. We will never know exactly what it meant to the early Native American. The spelling appears several other ways: Wakenda, Wakonda, Wyaconda.

Wah-Sha-She Prairie (Jasper). Wah-sha-she is an attempt to write phonetically one name for the Osage tribe. See Osage River.

Wainwright (Callaway). Platted in 1892 as a railroad town, Wainwright was originally called Linkville. During railroad construction, its name changed after Ellis Wainwright, a St. Louis capitalist (BD).

Wakenda [WAW kuhn daw] (Carroll). See Wah-Kon-Tah. P.O. 1876-now. Pop. 89.

Wakenda Creek (Carroll). First called Yellow Creek, the name was changed (RF). See Wah-Kon-Tah.

Wakonda State Park (Lewis). See Wah-Kon-Tah.

Wallace (Buchanan). This was named for an officer of the railroad (RF). P.O. 1877-1966. Pop. 50.

Wallstreet (Dallas). This mocking name was given by locals and accepted by the post office (LI). P.O. 1902-1907.

Wappapello
Washington State Park

Wappapello [WAH puh pel uh] (Wayne). This town was named by the president of the Frisco Railroad for Wapelillese, a friendly Native American chief. His name apparently meant "white bird." A similar form, *wapello*, is supposed to be the word for "chief." Wapelillese was friendly to Americans and moved peacefully west when they asked his people to abandon tribal lands (RF). P.O. 1884-now.

Warren County [WAH ruhn] or [WAW ruhn]. This county was named for General Joseph Warren, who urged that the Colonies rebel against Great Britain. He fell at the Battle of Bunker Hill in 1775. Organized 1833. Pop. 19,534.

Warrensburg (Johnson). In 1833, Martin Warren, a Kentuckian and Revolutionary War veteran, settled here (VR). Today, Warren's fame has been all but forgotten, eclipsed by a famous foxhound. A sculpture of the dog stands in front of the courthouse, and people remember the 19th-century case when "Old Drum" was killed by a farmer's neighbor. Missouri Senator George Graham Vest, a Democrat, Civil War veteran and great public orator, won damages for the bereaved owner by the force of his closing argument, "Eulogy on a Dog." The case went all the way to the U. S. Supreme Court. P.O. 1837-now. Pop. 15,244.

Warrenton (Warren) county seat. Banners on the light posts proclaim this a"City for All Seasons." It is named for the county. P.O. 1836-now. Pop. 3,596.

Warsaw (Benton) county seat. This name was chosen in admiration for the capital city of Poland. Poland had attempted an uprising against Russia in the 1830s (RF). P.O. 1839-now. Pop. 1,696.

Washington [WAH shing tuhn] or [WAW shing tuhn] (Franklin). The official name honors the father of our country (LI). The "Corn Cob Pipe Capital of the World," this old German town was occasionally called Owensville in honor of its founder, who was killed in a duel before the town was finished (RF). P.O. 1837, 1840-now. Pop. 10,704.

Washington County. This is the sixth oldest county in Missouri; it was named for President George Washington. Organized 1813. Pop. 20,380.

Washington State Park (Washington). The park is named for the county.

Water (Oregon). Streams here, it was said, were never dry. There are springs to feed them in all seasons (RF). P.O. 1898-1905.

Waterloo (Clark). Tradition says that a French man who fought with Napoleon lived here, OR, that the town was named because it is near excellent water facilities (RF). Once a coal-mining village (CG), this town was the county seat from 1836 to 1846, and again from 1854 to 1865. Each time the "City of the Classic Fox" (it's near the Fox River) experienced growth and prestige. It completely declined when the county seat was fixed at Kahoka. See Napoleon. P.O. (Clark) 1837-1876, (Lafayette) 1877-1909.

Watson (Atchison). This is the northwesternmost town in Missouri, situated in the rich corn country along the Missouri River where Missouri adjoins Nebraska and Iowa. It was named for an engineer on the Burlington Railroad (RF). P.O. 1869-1965. Pop. 137.

Waverly (LaFayette). First called Middletown (VR), which was already in use in the state, the storekeeper offered a free dress pattern to any lady if she could come up with a name. One lady, a reader of Sir Walter Scott novels, suggested Waverly. "So it goes," said the storekeeper, "Waverly it is" (CG). Others say the name is from Waverly, Illinois (RF). Previous post offices had used the name: (Lincoln) 1822-1833, (Rives) 1841-unknown, (Henry) unknown-1845, 1849-1852, (Lafayette) 1854-now. Pop. 837.

Wayne County [WAYN]. This county was organized early and named for General Anthony "Mad Anthony" Wayne, Revolutionary War hero. He was associated with Nathaniel Greene (see Greene County) and is remembered for establishing a line of forts from the east westward, punctuated by Fort Wayne, Indiana (RF). Organized 1818. Pop. 11,543.

Waynesville (Pulaski) county seat. This is named for Anthony Wayne. See Wayne County. P.O. 1834-now. Pop. 3,207.

Weaubleau Creek [WAH bloh]. First called the Lime River, this tributary of the Osage uses a French spelling for a Native American name. Sometimes spelled Wablo and Weablo, the original meaning has been lost (RF). A town in Hickory County, first called Haran for the Biblical site where Abraham lived, took the name Weaubleau City, then shortened it to Weaubleau. The name was also used by a town in Saint Clair County 1853-1867. P.O. Weaubleau City 1876-1880, Weaubleau 1881-now. Pop. 436.

Webb City
West Plains

Webb City (Jasper). As he plowed his field in 1873, John C. Webb ran over a chunk of lead. Two years later, a stick of dynamite opened the ground, and Webb left farming to become a developer. Zinc was also discovered here (VR). P.O. 1876-now. Pop. 7,449.

Webster County [WEB stuhr]. This county name honors the brilliant Daniel Webster, political leader, who died in 1852. Organized 1855. Pop. 23,753.

Webster Groves (St. Louis). Webster College was established here by a New Englander; the name honors Daniel Webster. When the post office was established, the "Groves" was added because another Webster existed in the state. P.O. 1862-1901. Pop. 22,992.

Weldon Spring (St. Charles). This town is named for John and Joseph Weldon, early residents (VR). It is also called Weldon Springs. John Weldon came to this area in 1796 with a Spanish land grant for 425 acres, including the spring for which Weldon Spring was named. Nearly 150 years later, during World War II, the federal government acquired almost 17,000 acres in the area for the construction of a munitions plant. In 1948, the property (except for the munitions plant) was given to the University of Missouri for an agricultural experiment station. The Conservation Department purchased 7,230 acres from the University in 1978. The acquisition brought the total acreage of Weldon Spring, Howell Island and August A. Busch Memorial conservation areas to 16,918 acres (BD). P.O. 1875-1957. Pop. 1,470.

Wellington (Lafayette). Once a coal-mining village (CG), the name was probably given for the Duke of Wellington who defeated Napoleon at Waterloo (RF). Napoleon and Waterloo are both nearby. Today, it's just a "spit on the road" (LI). P.O. 1840-now. Pop. 779.

Wentzville (St. Charles). This post office was named in honor of Mr. Wentz, chief engineer of the St. Louis, Kansas City and Northern Railroad. P.O. 1859-now. Pop. 5,088.

West Plains (Howell) county seat. This was named by its surveyor, who noted that it was west of the nearest town and located in grassy plains. When the county was organized, it was the only sizable settlement. All county records were burned during the Civil War, and postal delivery was suspended, but the town grew rapidly afterward. P.O. 1848-1864, 1866-now. Pop. 8,913.

Weston (Platte). This charming town near the Missouri River grew up rapidly and was named as settlers rushed to the west. Known early for foxhounds, bourbon, hemp and tobacco (VR), it was also the first town to ship goods to the Mormon capital of Salt Lake City (CG). P.O. 1838-now. Pop. 1,528.

Westphalia [west FAYL yuh] (Osage). Named for Westphalia, Germany, this town was founded by a priest who lasted seven years. Posted to his door, he left a note in Latin. Translated, it read, "Why would the man who courts hardships hie to the dusky Indies? Let him come to Westphalia and he will find hardships aplenty" (Enc). P.O. 1848-now. Pop. 287.

Westport (Jackson). Westport was founded at a time when large numbers of people were moving west. It was planned by business leaders who thought its natural river landing would make it the perfect port. The founders were right. In five months of 1859, 1,970 wagons, 840 horses, 4,000 mules, 15,000 oxen and 2,300 men passed through here to find new lives. In 1864, the Battle of Westport was the last Civil War battle west of the Mississippi. P.O. 1834-1902, now part of Kansas City.

Wet Glaze (Camden). This post office name misspells Wet Auglaize, a creek that never went dry (RF). See Auglaize Creek. P.O. 1848-1883, 1885-1938.

Wheatland (Hickory). This Ozarks town was probably named for the home of President James Buchanan near Lancaster, Pennsylvania, like other Wheatlands in the United States. The town was planned the year after he died. P.O. (Morgan) 1854-1864, (Hickory) 1867-now. Pop. 363.

Whistling Cave (Franklin). If the wind currents and water level are just right, this cave sounds a whistle (RF).

White Bear (Marion). This little town was named by a lime company. Their product was named for their location on Bear Creek and the white lime found here (RF).

White River. This large river, its water filtered by the wooded hills, naturally ran very clear. It was first called Unica (meaning "white") by Cherokees, then Rio Blanco by the Spaniards, Riviere au Blanc by the French; the name was translated literally into English (RF).

Whitecorn
Wilhelmina

Whitecorn (St. Charles). This part of the county was famous for growing white corn, a variety of which was named St. Charles (LI).

Who'd-a-thought-it (Pemiscot). This pioneer place disappeared in the early 1900s, but the name is remembered by a few around here. It probably means "Who would have thought anyone would live here?" (RF).

Whoop Up (Boone). Never more than a country store, there are at least four stories about the unusual town name. One tells that it was a busy place, and the proprietor made up the name in a particularly frenzied moment of waiting on customers. Or, this was a center for marble playing, a way to whoop it up in the old days (RF). Or, the name came from the owners of horse-drawn carts, who had to whoop their carts up the hill into town especially if they were carrying a load (LI). Another resident explained it this way, "Those Easley boys coined the phrase. They used to come into town to 'whoop it up,' or have a good time," she said. The name, pronounced [HOOP-up], has echoed through these hollers for over a century (BD).

Whosau Trace (St. Charles). An old trail that ran parallel with the Boonslick Trail into Osage Indian country, this is another phonetic spelling for the Native American tribal name (RF). See Osage River.

"Widow Creek" (Butler). This nickname was given to Spencer Creek because there were so many Civil War widows living there (RF).

Wien [WEEN] (Chariton). This is the true name of the capital of Bavaria, called by Americans "Vienna" (LI). P.O. 1873-1903.

Wigwam Branch (Morgan). This was a favorite hunting ground of the Osage Tribe (RF), named by Americans.

Wild Cat Branch. There are three creeks so-named. Along with two caves, one hill, five hollows and one mountain, which testifies there once were many cougars, also called mountain lions or wild cats, in our state (LI).

Wilderness (Oregon). See Irish Settlement. P.O. 1882-1954.

Wilhelmina [wil uh MEE nuh] (Dunklin). This settlement was settled by Germans and named for the Queen of Holland (RF). P.O. 1911-1957.

Williamsburg (Callaway). The first post office here was called Fruits, the name of the postmaster. When the post office moved to the home of Harvey Williams, the name was changed (RF). P.O. 1835-now.

Willow Springs (Howell). This town, first known as Rowe Spring, now bears a descriptive name given for the tree growing nearby (RF). P.O. 1869-now. Pop. 2,038.

Wilson's Creek Battlefield (Christian). Local folks called this site Wilson Creek, naming it for the landowner, James Wilson. The "'s" probably came with Union troops who were not familiar with the local name. Some Union company flags used "Wilson's" rather than "Wilson." The National Park is Missouri's most important Civil War battlefield.

U.S. Board on Geographic Names

A s the country was populated by people of diverse backgrounds, confusion arose over the meanings of words and the correct names for places. Everyday conversation allowed people to refer to places in many ways: by their owners' names, their geographical location, their history or some other distinction. Places often had two or three names, and just as many spellings and pronunciations.

An early effort to standardize place names came with the 1804 Lewis and Clark expedition. As they mapped their route along the Missouri River, they used English names for landmarks even if names of other languages were commonly used. Fortunately, common usage prevailed, so the Pomme de Terre River never really became known as Wild Potatoe Creek and Auxvasse Creek never really became known as Muddy River.

Despite the early efforts to standardize usage, new Americans struggled with the language. Friedrich Schmidt warned Germans against buying land in the "bottoms." "Bottoms are areas that are flooded by rivers," he said. Gottfried Duden countered that "Bottoms signifies nothing else but the valley plains of streams, rivers and brooks which are no more in danger of floods than the river valleys of Germany."   *continued*

U.S. Board on Geographic Names
continued

Who was right? It depended on local language and the persuasion of the observer. A small waterway might be labeled a creek, crik, branch, stream, streamlet, draw, run, fork, brook, race, channel, bayou or river, depending on who was doing the calling. If the year was dry, it could be called a ditch, trench or dry creek.

In 1890, the U.S. Board on Geographic Names was created. The mission of the board is "to establish and maintain uniform geographic name usage throughout the Federal Government." In its early years, the board simply sought to standardize name usage on government maps and to avoid duplication. New names, needed for reference or given to commemorate something, were evaluated as to "appropriateness, acceptability and need." Today, offensive and derogatory names can be brought before the board.

Some standardizations result in names that seem wrong to local people. Punkin Center is marked with signs that say "Pumpkin Center." Wilson Creek goes by "Wilson's Creek." Pine Run, a complete place name to those who use "run" as a synonym for "creek," has officially been changed to Pine Run Creek. Mormon's Fork has been, for the same reason, changed to Mormon's Fork Creek.

Despite these problems, standardization has been good for the most part. Today, maps, post offices and the highway department all agree on the names of most places.

Winchester. Probably named for Winchester, Virginia (RF), the name has been claimed by two post offices. It prevailed in New Madrid County from 1813 to 1822, and in Clark County from 1840 to 1905. Now the name is used by a village in St. Louis County. Pop. 1,678.

Wire Road. This road, approximately following the line of U.S. Highway 66, established the path for a telegraph wire from Rolla to Springfield during the Civil War (RF).

Wisdom (Benton). Named for A.J. Wisdom, a local (RF). P.O. 1897-1956.

Wittenberg (Perry). First called Stephan's Landing for their pastor, the founders changed the name when he was accused of improprieties. A man with great expectations, he had planned to build a city called Stephansburg and a university called Stephan's College. After the scandal, many of his followers returned to Germany. Others stayed, renaming the settlement after the German city where Martin Luther declared his separation from the Catholic church (RF). See Altenburg. P.O. 1862-now. Pop. 300.

Wolf Island (Mississippi). Named for the animal, this island village sits on the Missouri side of the Mississippi River, across from Kentucky. For many years, the island itself was claimed by one state, then the other. Today it belongs to Kentucky (LI). P.O. 1846-1860, 1868-now.

Worlds of Fun. Rides in this amusement park are named such things as Orient Express and Zambini Zinger to keep with the theme based on Jules Verne's book Around the World in Eighty Days (LI).

Worth County [WUHRTH]. Named for General William J. Worth, this was one of the counties reduced in size when Iowa gained statehood, following a bitterly contested border dispute. The dispute and U.S. Supreme Court case is known as The Honey War of 1838. Organized 1861. Pop. 2,440.

Wright City [REYET] (Warren). Named for a local man who served as state representative and state senator, a 1995 billboard proclaims this town is "the Gateway to Country Living." As St. Louis spreads westward along I-70, it is becoming a commuters' suburb (LI). P.O. 1858-now. Pop. 1,250.

Wright County. The county was named for U.S. Senator Silas Wright, a Democrat and statesman of the day. Organized 1841. Pop. 16,758.

Wyaconda River [weye uh KAHN duh]. This lovely place name is Native American, designating a place favored by the Deity (VR). The river has a legend: At its mouth was once found a pair of Sioux who had died without a mark on them. Their strange deaths suggested that the site may be inhabited by the All-powerful (RF). See Wah-kon-tah. Towns along the river have taken its name. P.O. (Scotland) 1850-1874, (Clark) 1888-now.

Wyreka (Putnam). Named for Yreka, California, the postmaster used a different spelling (GS). P.O. 1854.

Xenia
Yukon

Xenia. There have been two Missouri towns named for the Ohio town. One of the first towns was in Nodaway County, it went out of business (RF). P.O. 1857-1872. A few years later, Lemen in Putnam County changed its name to Xenia (APM). P.O. 1879-1898. The original Greek meaning of *xenia* is "friendly hospitality."

Yarrow (Adair). An old coal-mining town along the banks of the Chariton River (CG), this was named for a river in Scotland (RF). P.O. 1904-unknown.

Yolo (Gentry). Two stories: (1) The postmaster here painted his house a bright yellow. The 20x60 structure was a grand two-story, four-room building with a large porch to protect stage coach riders as they entered. In its later years it became a hay barn (LI). (2) The name came from Yolo County, California, where many Missourians went during the Gold Rush. Some folks say that the son of the postmaster here joined the Gold Rush and picked up his mail in Yolo, so the postmaster named his place to maintain the tie (LI). P.O. 1855-1868.

Yukon [yoo KAHN] (Texas). (1) The name is Athapascan for "the river" (JL). (2) The name was chosen by vote of the community. Gold had recently been discovered in Alaska and Yukon was in the news (RF). P.O. 1899-now.

Z

Zalma [ZAL muh] (Bollinger). This town is named for Zalma Block, friend of a railroad builder (GS). P.O. 1890-now. Pop. 83.

Zanoni [zan OH nee] (Ozark). This post office was named for an 1843 novel by Edward Bulwer Lytton (GS). P.O. 1898-1927, 1930-now.

Zebra (Camden). Some say this town was named for striped rocks on the bluffs (LI), but it was probably named after a person named Ziebar (RF). Today, Zebra lies under the Lake of the Ozarks. P.O. 1886-1935.

Zell (Ste. Genevieve). Before the Civil War, this town was called The German Settlement and it still has pride in its German heritage. There are Zells in many parts of Germany and nobody knows which Zell this one refers to (LI). P.O. 1881-1922. Pop. 100.

Zeta (Stoddard). Named by a classics lover for the sixth letter of the Greek alphabet, this was the place where a little group of believers went to wait for Judgment Day on March 1, 1914 (LI). P.O. 1895-1896, 1907-1936.

Zewapeta [zuh WAH puh tuh] (Scott). See Tywappity Bottoms.

Zig (Adair). This was named for a popular citizen, Harrison Ziegler (RF). P.O. 1870-1908.

Zonker (Douglas). This post office bore the family name of the postmaster (RF).

Zumwalt's Fort (St. Charles). This early fort provided shelter for local families in time of attack. It was named for Jacob Zumwalt (RF).

Zwanzig [ZWAN zig] (Morgan). This name, meaning "twenty" in German, was given for a local man, August Zwanzig (RF). P.O. 1892-1901.

Index

Index

This index begins with a separate listing of Missouri counties.

Counties

Index

Index

U

U.S. Board on Geographic Names
191, 192

V

Vernon 2, 8, 26, 65, 110, 120,
122, 124, 165, 166, 183, 184

W

Warren 13, 44, 45, 48, 49, 71, 75,
77, 90, 91, 105, 137, 165,
178, 186, 193
Washington, George 31, 46, 88, 104,
122, 186
World War I 17, 74, 79, 85, 116,
139
World War II 46, 74, 188
Worth 68, 147, 168, 193

About the Author

Margot Ford McMillen was born and raised in Chicago and the suburbs, received her B.A. from Northwestern University in Evanston, Illinois, and moved to Missouri in 1972. She has lived in Missouri ever since, and has raised two daughters in Callaway County. She has also devoted herself to learning and writing about the folklife of the state.

McMillen's earliest articles appeared in the St. Louis and Kansas City newspapers, and since then she has written for national quilting magazines, farming magazines and old-time music magazines. She received her M.A. in English from the University of Missouri-Columbia in 1987.

McMillen's book The Masters and Their Traditional Arts and a series of brochures on Missouri traditions were published by the Missouri Cultural Heritage Center at the University of Missouri-Columbia in 1986. From 1988 to 1994, she published Our Missouri, a quarterly journal for elementary students studying Missouri history and culture. She is a regular contributor to the Missouri Conservationist.

In 1994, the University of Missouri Press published her book Paris, Tightwad, and Peculiar: Missouri Place Names as part of its Missouri Heritage Readers Series. In 1995, she was invited by the Secretary of State Rebecca Cook to write the keynote essay on childhood for the Missouri Blue Book, the state manual.

McMillen teaches critical thinking for the English Department at Westminster College in Fulton and lives on a farm in Callaway County. She is married to Professor Howard Marshall of the University of Missouri-Columbia Department of Art and Archaeology. On their farm, they raise Salers cattle and enjoy a varying selection of dogs, cats, horses, hogs and chickens.

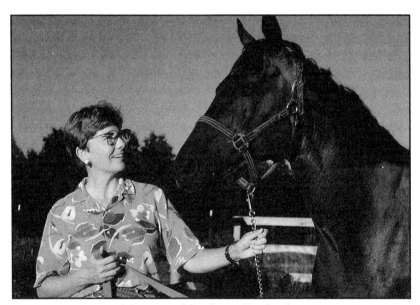
Margot and her horse Benjamin.

The Show Me Missouri Series

99 Fun Things To Do
in Columbia & Boone County

ISBN: 0-9646625-2-3

Guide to 99 hidden highlights, unique dining, galleries, museums, towns, people and history in Columbia, Rocheport, Centralia and Boone County. Most trips are free or under $10. Includes maps, photos, accessibility of sites. Fully indexed. 168 pages. By Pamela Watson. $12.95

√A to Z Missouri

ISBN: 0-9646625-4-X

Abo to Zwanzig! A dictionary-style book of Missouri place name origins. Includes history for each town and community, pronunciations, population, county, post office dates and more. 220 pages. By Margot Ford McMillen. $14.95

Best of Missouri Hands

ISBN: 0-9646625-5-8

Profiles of Missouri's fine artists and craftsmen. From porcelain to wood and pewter to gold, *Best of Missouri Hands* shows the best our state has to offer. This book highlights many traditional art forms and techniques, and the artists behind the expressions. 152 pages. By Brett Dufur. $12.95

Exploring Missouri Wine Country

ISBN: 0-9646625-6-6

This guidebook to Missouri Wine Country offers an intimate look at Missouri's winemakers and wineries, including how to get there, their histories and the story of how Missouri came to have its own Rhineland. Includes wine tips, recipes, home-brew recipes, dictionary of wine terms and more. Also lists nearby Bed and Breakfasts and lodging. 168 pages. By Brett Dufur. $14.95

Famous Missourians Who Made History

ISBN: 0-9646625-9-0

A book of easily digestible history, for school children and adults alike, of short stories and humorous comic-style illustrations of more than 50 Missourians who made a contribution to the state or nation. Compiled by Brett Dufur. $14.95

Forgotten Missourians Who Made History

ISBN: 0-9646625-8-2

A book of short stories and humorous comic-style illustrations of more than 50 Missourians who made a contribution to the state or nation yet are largely forgotten by subesquent generations. Companion book to *Famous Missourians Who Made History*. Compiled by Jim Borwick and Brett Dufur. $14.95

The Complete Katy Trail Guidebook
ISBN: 0-9646625-0-7

The most complete guide to services, towns, people, places and history along Missouri's 200-mile Katy Trail. This updated edition covers the cross-state hiking and biking trail from Clinton to St. Charles — now America's longest rails-to-trails project. Includes trailhead maps, 80 photos, Flood of '93, how to make blueberry wine, uses for Missouri mud and more. 168 pages. By Brett Dufur. $14.95

What's That?
ISBN: 0-9646625-1-5

A Nature Guide to the Missouri River Valley

Companion guide to the *Katy Trail Guidebook*. This easy-to-use, illustrated four-season guide identifies trees, flowers, birds, animals, insects, rocks, fossils, clouds, reptiles, footprints and more. Features the Missouri River Valley's most outstanding sites and nature daytrips. 176 pages. Compiled by Brett Dufur. $14.95

Wit & Wisdom
ISBN: 0-9646625-3-1

of Missouri's Country Editors

A compilation of over 600 pithy sayings from pioneer Missouri newspapers. Many of these quotes and quips date to the 19th century yet remain timely for today's readers. Richly illustrated and fully indexed to help you find that perfect quote. 168 pages. By William Taft. $14.95

Pebble Publishing

P.O. Box 431 ❖ Columbia, MO 65205-0431
(800) 576-7322 ❖ Fax: (573) 698-3108

Quantity	Book Title	x Unit Price =	Total

Mo. residents add 6.975% sales tax = ------------

Shipping ($1.24 each book) x = ------------

Total = ------------

Name:_____

Address:_____ Apt._____

City, State, Zip_____

Phone: (_____) _____

Credit Card # _____

Expiration Date _____/_____/_____ Please send catalog _____

Visit *Trailside Books* online at http://www.trailsidebooks.com

JUNE 27, 2008

how Me Missouri books are available at many local bookstores. They can also be ordered directly from the publisher, using this form, or ordered by phone, fax or over the Internet.

Pebble Publishing also distributes 100 other books of regional interest, rails-to-trails, Missouri history, heritage, nature, recreation and more. These are available through our online bookstore and mail-order catalog. Visit our online bookstore, called *Trailside Books* at http://www.trailsidebooks.com, or leave a message at brett@trailsidebooks.com. If you would like to receive our catalog, please fill out and mail the form on the previous page.